THE MORMON TRAIL

Yesterday and Today

William E. Hill

Utah State University Press
Logan, Utah
1996

To
George, Jenille, and
their grandson Matthew,
good friends met along the way

Typography by WolfPack
  Cover design by Michelle Sellers

Library of Congress Cataloging-in-Publication Data

Hill, William E.
    The Mormon Trail : yesterday and today / William E. Hill.
        p. cm.
    Includes bibliographical references and index.
    ISBN 0-87421-202-2
    1. Mormon Trail. 2. Mormons—West (U.S.)—History. 3. West (U.S.)—
History. I. Title.
    F593.H553 1996
    978—dc20   95-50223
                                                                    CIP

Contents

Illustrations

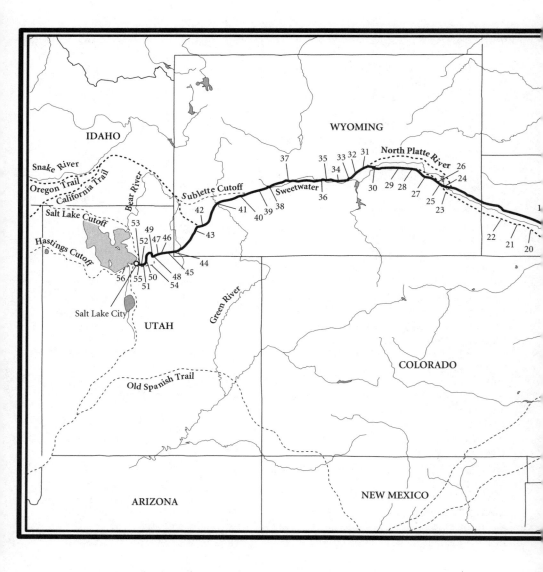

THE MORMON NATIONAL HISTORIC TRAIL MAP SITES

1. Carthage
2. Nauvoo
3. Keokuk
4. Garden Grove
5. Mt. Pisgah
6. Coralville
7. Fort Des Moines
8. Council Bluffs (Kanes-
   ville) area
9. Winter Quarters/
   Omaha Area

10. Fort Leavenworth
11. Elkhorn Ferry
12. Loup Ferry
13. Lone Tree
14. Pawnee Village
15. Wood River
16. Fort Kearny
17. Ash Hollow
18. Indian Lookout
19. Ancient Bluff Ruins
20. Courthouse Rock

21. Chimney Rock
22. Scotts Bluff
23. Fort Laramie
24. Mexican Hill
25. Register Cliffs & Trail
    Ruts
26. Laramie Peak
27. Sidley Peak
28. Red Hills
29. Black Hills

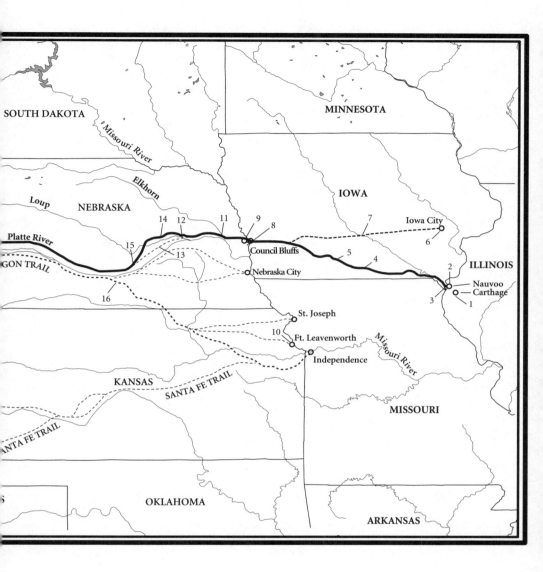

Preface

MY OTHER BOOKS ABOUT THE OREGON, CALIFORNIA, AND SANTA FE Trails were primarily concerned with the historical development of the physical route of the trails and their condition today. This book on the Mormon Trail, however, must be expanded to include not only that type of information but also material about the development of the Mormon faith and church. The reader must have some general knowledge of the history of the Mormon Church, officially known as the Church of Jesus Christ of Latter-day Saints, in order to understand the development of the Mormon Trail since the history of the two are intertwined. This book is not an in-depth explanation of the major tenets of the Mormon faith and its different branches. It is, however, a book that is meant to serve as an introduction and overview of the Mormon Trail experience and to spark an interest in further research and study of its different aspects and influences on the development of the United States. Some of the practices and beliefs associated with the early Mormon Church and its society will be identified later in order to give the reader a clearer understanding of the development of the Mormon Trail.

Today the use of the term "Mormon Trail" is usually synonymous with the route designated by the National Park Service as the Mormon Pioneer National Historic Trail. There are also other trails with National Historic Trail status: the Oregon National Historic Trail, the California National Historic Trail, the Santa Fe National Historic Trail, and the Pony Express National Historic Trail. In 1978 the Oregon Trail was the first to receive this designation during the resurgence of interest in western migration. By the mid-1980s the National Park Service had conducted its historic resource study, identifying and mapping the Oregon Trail route. The Mormon Trail was also designated a National Historic Trail then, but it has only been in the last few years that its historic resource study was completed and detailed mapping commenced. The other three trails have received their national historic trail designation in recent years. Other historic routes, such as the Mormon Battalion route, are also being considered for this status.

By necessity the specific routes of these National Historic Trails have been narrowed down from all the actual routes used by all the different emigrants. The particular route of the respective emigrants often varied from one year to another or even from month to month. Sometimes these trail variations consisted of only a few feet, at other times parallel routes miles apart developed, and short cuts which were heavily used one year might be all but forgotten in subsequent years. To have included every twist and turn, every parallel route and camp road, every short cut developed or ever used by emigrants during the period of westward migration would have been an impossible task for the National Park Service to have accomplished.

Emigrants also used a variety of locations for outfitting and jumping off. For the Mormons during 1846, it was Nauvoo, Illinois, and the next year, Winter Quarters, Nebraska. For the next twenty years it could have been one or more of a variety of additional cities or towns such as Kanesville, Iowa; Westport, Missouri; Iowa City, Iowa; or Wyoming, Nebraska. The route that has been designated the Mormon Pioneer National Historic Trail itself was also used extensively by many emigrants going to Oregon and California. Merrill Mattes and other prominent western historians note that the trail on the north side of the Platte, although presently designated the Mormon Trail, was known by other names, such as the Council Bluffs Road, and it was used by many more emigrants going to Oregon and California than by those Mormons going to Utah during the period of westward migration. This does not, however, diminish the concept of a Mormon Trail and its significance, but only helps to better explain the concept of National Historic Trails.

Depending on the year, emigrants of all kinds, with different destinations as their goal, could be found traveling together along parts of the same route. This was especially true of the eastern portions of the trail. Traders and emigrants to Santa Fe, to California, to Oregon, or to Salt Lake City used the Independence, Missouri, area as their outfitting and jumping-off site. St. Joseph, Missouri, was used heavily by travelers to California and Oregon and only briefly by the Mormons and the Pony Express. Council Bluffs, Iowa—the Kanesville area then—was heavily used by early trappers, and by California-, Oregon-, and Salt Lake- and Great Basin area-bound emigrants. The central Platte River Valley in Nebraska and parts of the trails in Wyoming were used by all those going to Oregon, California, or Salt Lake City, and with the opening of the Bozeman Trail even those going to Montana could be found sharing the same route, traveling side by side. The reality of the trails was that there really was no one single route that was exclusively used all the way by any one category of emigrants. Some segments of the trails may have been used predominantly by travelers to one destination, especially towards the end of the trails. However, through the years all the trails overlapped, and the travelers intermingled with one another.

In this book the term Mormon Trail will refer to the 1,300 mile route designated the Mormon Pioneer National Historic Trail. The route starts from Nauvoo, Illinois, and goes west across Iowa through Council Bluffs, Iowa, to Winter Quarters in Omaha, Nebraska. The trail then follows along the north side of the Platte River, crossing the North Platte River to the south side near Fort Laramie.

There appear to be three factors that influenced the original decision of the Mormons to use the trail on the north side of the Platte River. The fact that Winter Quarters was established on the north side of the Platte made it most likely that the Mormons would travel on that side. In addition, since the south side was more heavily traveled, there was the contention that they would be less likely to suffer persecution. Also, grasses were more plentiful since fewer people and animals were using the north side.

Near Fort Laramie the Mormon Trail crosses the North Platte River. Then it generally follows the south side of the North Platte until it again crosses the river near present-day Casper, Wyoming. There the trail cuts across to meet and follow the Sweetwater River to the South Pass area. Turning southwest, the trail heads down the Big Sandy, across the Green River, and over to Fort Bridger. This major section coincides with the Oregon National Historic Trail and parts of the California National Historic Trail. From Fort Bridger the Mormon Trail continues in a southwesterly direction down into Echo Canyon to the Weber River and over the Wasatch Mountains into the Valley of the Great Salt Lake. The majority of the route west of Fort Bridger had been first used by those emigrants following the Hastings Cutoff going to California in 1846. It was the Donner-Reed Party that cut the wagon route over the Wasatch Mountains. This whole route represents the one used by the Mormon pioneers in 1846-48. As mentioned earlier, many of the Mormons who came in later years often followed portions of other routes, which varied depending on the year they traveled. This fact will become evident when you read some of the diaries listed in the bibliography as they describe different areas and the specific routes they took. The map included in this book shows the Mormon Pioneer National Historic Trail route along with some of the other National Historic Trails and many of the other cutoffs and feeder trails.

In recent years there have been several trail organizations that have become heavily involved in preserving these great emigrant trails. The Oregon-California Trails Association (OCTA) was founded in 1982 when some historians and trail buffs came together to see what they could do to save the Oregon Trail. It quickly developed into an organization dedicated to not only the Oregon and California Trails but to all the major emigrant trails. Its headquarters are located in Independence, Missouri, at the National Frontier Trails Center. OCTA has succeeded, and today it is the largest of all the national historic trail preservation groups. In addition to the national organization, it has local chapters in all the western trail states. Members, however, can be found as far away as Japan in the Far East and Germany in Europe. It has actively supported the National Historic Trails status of the Oregon, Santa Fe, Mormon, California, and Pony Express Trails. OCTA is also supporting the designation and addition of other trails into the National Historic Trail system. It has worked on its own and with the assistance of the National Parks Service (NPS) and the Bureau of Land Management (BLM) to map and mark the trails on both private and public lands.

Another group that has worked extensively to have the Mormon Trail designated as a National Historic Trail is the Mormon Trails Association. This organization was founded in 1992. Its headquarters are in Salt Lake City. It has been working extensively with the National Parks Service on the Mormon Trail survey. The organization also has a number of state and local chapters. It has been very active in recent years researching and developing the sites with historical significance in Mormon history. Many of these sites seem to have been long forgotten, but now they are getting the attention they have long deserved.

The two major branches of the Mormon Church, the Church of Jesus Christ of Latter-day Saints, with its headquarters in Salt Lake City, Utah, and the Reorganized Church of Jesus Christ of Latter Day Saints, with its headquarters in Independence, Missouri, have been active in obtaining and restoring sites of historical significance to the Mormon faith for many years. Historic Nauvoo, Illinois, is a prime example of their longtime and continuing work, but there are also many other sites that have been saved by either or both churches. The "This is the Place" state park along with its "Old Deseret" village is another area undergoing extensive expansion by the state of Utah through the Utah Statehood Centennial Commission.

Just as the history of the Mormon Trail is intertwined with the other emigrant trails, the history of the Mormons and Utah are also interwoven. The committees responsible for the celebrations of both the sesquicentennial of the Mormon Trail and the centennial of Utah's statehood have brought about a flurry of activities, too many to mention all. Some projects are presently in the planning stage, others are well on their way to completion, and many have been recently finished.

All of these organizations have made it much easier for the modern traveler to experience the Mormon Trail. Yet two other significant pieces of Mormon history must be mentioned again. They are the songs "Come, Come, Ye Saints" and "The Handcart Song." The verses of these two songs tell us more about the Mormon Trail experience than perhaps many of the diaries that were kept by the Mormon emigrants. In the songs are the stories of their hopes, their pain and suffering, and the final fulfillment of their dreams. "Come, Come, Ye Saints" was written by William Clayton on April 16, 1846 while camped at Locust Creek, Iowa, during the Mormon exodus from Nauvoo, Illinois. "The Handcart Song" reflects a later period in their history when thousands of Mormons were determined to reach Zion/Salt Lake City.

Read their words again, and then start your journey west along the Mormon Trail.

Come, Come, Ye Saints—1846

William Clayton

Come, Come, ye Saints, no toil nor labor fear, But with joy wend your way;
Tho' hard to you this journey may appear, Grace shall be as your day.
'Tis better far for us to strive Our useless cares from
us to drive; Do this, and joy your hearts will swell—All is well! all is well!

Why should we mourn, or think our lot is hard? 'Tis not so; all is right!
Why should we think to earn a great reward, If we now shun the fight?
Gird up your loins, fresh courage take, Our God will never
us forsake; And soon we'll have this truth to tell—All is well! all is well!

We'll find the place which God for us prepared, Far a-way in the West;
Where none shall come to hurt or make a-fraid; There the Saints will be blessed.
We'll make the air with music ring—Shout prais-es to our
God and King; Above the rest these words we'll tell—All is well! all is well!

And should we die before our journey's through, Hap-py day! all is well!
We then are free from toil and sor-row too; With the just we shall dwell.
But if our lives are spared again To see the Saints, their
rest ob-tain, O how we'll make this chorus swell—All is well! all is well!

The Handcart Song—1851

John D. T. McAllister

Ye Saints that dwell on Europe's
    shores,
Prepare yourselves with many more
To leave behind your native land
For sure God's Judgements are at
    hand,
Prepare to cross the stormy main
And with the faithful make a start
To cross the plains with your hand-
    cart.

Chorus:

For some must push and some must
    pull,
As we go marching up the hill.
So merrily on the way we go,
Until we reach the Valley, Oh!

That land that boasts of liberty
You ne'er again may wish to see
While poor men toil to earn their
    bread
And rich men are much better fed,
And people boast of their great light.
You see they are as dark as night
And from them you must make a start
To cross the plains with our hand-
    carts.

Chorus

But some will say it is too bad
The Saints upon their feet to pad
And more than that to push a load
As they go marching up the road.
We say this is Jehovah's plan
To gather out the best of men,
And women too, for none but they
Will ever gather in this way.

Chorus

As on the way the carts are hurled
'T would very much surprise the world
To see the old and feeble dame
Lending her hand to push the same.
The young girls they will dance and
    sing.
The young men happier than a king,
The Children they will laugh and play
Their strength increasing day by day.

Chorus

But ere before the valley gained
We will be met upon the plains
With music sweet and friends so dear
And fresh supplies our hearts to
    cheer,
Then with the music and the song
How cheerfully we'll march along
So thankfully you make a start
To cross the plains with our hand-
    carts.

Chorus

When we get there amongst the rest
Industrious be and we'll be blessed,
And in our chambers be shut in
With Judgement cleanse the earth
    from sin,
For well we know it will be so,
God's servants spoke it long ago,
And tell us it's high time to start
To cross the plains with our hand-
    carts.

Chorus:

For some must push and some must
    pull,
As we go marching up the hill.
So merrily on the way we go,
Until we reach the Valley, Oh!

—from Hafen and Hafen,
Handcarts to Zion

Roster of the Pioneer Company to Utah, 1847

They are given as divided into companies of "Tens":

First Ten—Wilford Woodruff, captain; John S. Fowler, Jacob D. Burnham, Orson Pratt, Joseph Egbert, John Freeman, Marcus B. Thorpe, George A. Smith, George Wardle

Second Ten—Ezra T. Benson, captain; Thomas B. Grover, Barbaras (Barnabas) L. Adams, Roswell Stevens, Amasa M. Lyman, Starling (Sterling) G. Driggs, Albert Carrington, Thomas Bullock, George Brown,Willard Richards, Jesse C. Little

Third Ten—Phineas H. Young, captain; John Y. Green, Thomas Tanner, Brigham Young, Addison Everett, Truman O. Angel(l), Lorenzo D. Young, Bryant Stringham, Joseph Scofield, Albert P. Rockford

Fourth Ten—Luke S. Johnson, captain; John Holman, Edmond Ellsworth (Elsworth), Alvarnus Hanks, George R. Grant, Millen Atwood, Samuel B. Fox, Tunis Rappleyee, Harry Pierce, William Kykes (Dykes), Jacob Weiler

Fifth Ten—Stephen H. Goddard, captain; Tarlton Lewis, Henry G. Sherwood, Zebedee Coltrin, Sylvester H. Earl, John Dixon, Samuel H. Marble, George Scholes, William Henrie, William. A. Empey

Sixth Ten—Charles Shumway, captain; Andrew Schumway, Thomas Woolsey, Chauncey Loveland, Erastus Snow, James Craig, William Wordsworth, William Vance, Simeon Howd, Seeley Owen

Seventh Ten—James Case, captain; Artemas Johnson, William C. A. Smoot, Franklin B. Dewey, William Carter, Franklin G. Losee, Burr Frost, Datus Ensign, Franklin Stewart, Monroe Frink, Eric Glines, Ozro Eastman

Eighth Ten—Seth Taft, captain; Horace Thorton, Stephen Kelsey, John S. Eldredge, Charles D. Barnum, Alma Williams, Rufus Allen, Robert T. Thomas, James W. Stewart, Elijah Newman, Levi N. Kendall, Francis Boggs, David Grant

Ninth Ten—Howard Egan, captain; Heber C. Kimball, William A. King, Thomas Cloward, Hosea Cushing, Robert Byard, George Billings, Edison Whipple, Philo Johnson, William Clayton

Tenth Ten—Appleton M. Harmon, captain; Carlos Murray, Horace K. Whitney, Orson K. Whitney, Orrin P.(Porter) Rockwell, Nathaniel T. (Thomas) Brown, R. Jackson Redding, John Pack, Francis Pomeroy, Aaron Farr, Nathaniel Fairbanks

Eleventh Ten—John S. Higbee, captain; John Wheeler, Solomon Chamberlain, Conrad Klineman, Joseph Rooker, Perry Fitzgerald, John H. Tippetts, James Davenport, Henson Walker, Benjamin Rolfe

Twelfth Ten—Norton Jacobs, captain; Charles A. Harper, George Woodward, Stephen Markham, Lewis Barney, George Mills, Andrew Gibbons, Joseph Hancock, John W. Norton

Thirteenth Ten—John Brown, captain; Shadrach Roundy, Levi Jackman, Lyman Curtis, Hans C. Hansen (Hanson), Mathew Ivory, David Powers, Hark Lay (African American), Oscar Crosby (African American)

Fourteenth Ten—Joseph Mathews, captain; Gilbroid Summe, John Gleason, Charles Burke, Alexander P. Chessley (Chesley), Rodney Badger, Norman Taylor, Green Flake (African American), Ellis Eames

Three women and two children also accompanied the camp. They were the wife of Lorenzo Young, Harriet, and their two children, Isaac and Sabisky; Clarissa Decker Young, one of Brigham's wives; and Ellen Sanders Kimball, one of Heber's wives.

Ellis Eames returned to Winter Quarters from the Pioneer camp the day after they left on account of sickness.

INTRODUCTION

The Nature of the Mormon Trail

THE MORMON TRAIL EXPERIENCE IS UNIQUE WHEN COMPARED WITH THE experiences of the other major trails of westward migration. Some of the characteristics associated with the Mormon Trail are similar to those of the other trails. When those characteristics are compared or discussed individually, it would seem to lead one to the conclusion that the trail experiences are the same, but it is the combination of those individual characteristics, along with other factors, that lead one to conclude that the nature of the Mormon Trail experience is unique. By examining the motivations, demographic characteristics, practices of the Mormons, planning and organization of the wagon companies, and the methods of transportation, this fact will become evident.

The reasons for the development of the Santa Fe, Oregon, and California Trails and the motivations of many of the emigrants were largely economic. The Santa Fe Trail, the earliest of the major westward trails, was developed in the 1820s primarily as a two-way trail of commerce, which was later used by emigrants. The traders were concerned with bringing needed trade goods from the United States and the Independence, Missouri, area to Santa Fe in Mexico. They knew that goods were scarce in Santa Fe and that large profits were possible. After trading there they would then return to the United States with cash and additional products to sell at a profit. For the first quarter century this was the major use of the Santa Fe Trail. The travelers were almost exclusively men, traders and their hired teamsters and, later, professional wagonmasters with their teamsters.

The emigrants who later began to use the Santa Fe Trail also did it for economic reasons. Some were emigrants traveling to the Southwest to settle in the area to make a new life for themselves. Many were gold seekers using the Santa Fe Trail as the first segment of their journey to California. From Santa Fe they might have taken a southern trail along the Gila River, or the Old Spanish Trail, which angled northwest from Santa Fe into Utah before turning southwesterly towards Nevada and California. The western section of the Old Spanish Trail was also later incorporated into a route that led from Salt Lake to California. It afforded California-bound emigrants and gold seekers another way west and also helped to open much of Utah and the Great Basin to settlement.

The 1840s brought the development of the Oregon and California Trails. They were originally developed primarily as emigrant trails, but generally followed the route and stopped at sites familiar to those of the earlier trappers and traders. The wagon trail to Oregon was primarily used by emigrants who wanted to settle in the fertile valleys. They had heard stories of the Oregon Territory and the free rich lands of the Willamette River Valley. Many left lands in the Midwest and the East, which had been in the midst of a recession. They left with the intent of traveling as quickly as possible and starting a new life. For the Gentiles, a term used by Mormons for all non-Mormons, the main driving force was to get to the lands of the West Coast. Once they arrived, there was really little concern for the route they used or its further improvements. It was envisioned as a one-way route.

The lands between their jumping-off and destination sites were seen as an obstacle to pass through with little concern for the area itself. Any stopping on the trail was temporary. Some emigrants noted areas which might prove to be rich farming areas, but they did not settle there. They quickly continued on their way to Oregon or California. Some emigrants, after building a raft or ferry to cross a river might stay for a day or two to ferry other emigrants across. This would enable them to earn some extra money for themselves, but then they too quickly moved on. Enoch Conyers, for example, earned $33.50 in one day and then proceeded on his journey. Samuel Barlow built a toll road over the Cascade Mountains at the end of the Oregon Trail to bypass the dangerous raft trip down the Columbia River to the Willamette River Valley. After he had gotten the money back it had cost him, he sold his interests in the road. Thus, it seems that many of the improvements made were primarily for the developers' benefit and were temporary at best.

The California Trail was also initially used by emigrants intent on starting a new life. Stories of the rich lands of California also provided the early and later emigrants with their motivation. However, the discovery of gold brought a different type of emigrant to California. Economics was still the motivation, but it was a short-term motive rather than a long-term one. They hoped to find gold, get rich, and return home to their families back east. However, the discovery of gold also brought tradesmen, shop owners, and farmers. These were the ones who really "struck it rich" by selling their products to the gold seekers. With the exception of some of the 49ers who hoped to strike it rich quickly and return to their families back east, the California Trail was mainly developed for one-way travel. Only after California became a territory and then a state did the trail develop into a two-way route with its expanded use by the military and the traders and professional teamsters hauling goods and supplies across the continent.

The gold fever of 1849 and the early 1850s also resulted in a noticeable change in the make-up of the trail travelers. Whereas some of the earlier emigrants included families, the majority of the travelers were now men. Many of the wagon companies, such as J. Goldsborough Bruff's Washington City and California Mining Association, and the pack trains were exclusively composed of men. The travelers to Oregon, however, remained largely composed of families. Rarely were single women found on the trails unless they were traveling with their parents. Respectable women, both single or married, it seems, did not travel alone.

Thus, for the major trails that existed prior to the Mormon Trail, the economic factor played the central role in their development. Only because of the repeated use and the two-way traffic on the Santa Fe Trail did the traders have a vested interest in making improvements, that is, any improvements that could reduce the time it took to travel back and forth. Also any reduction in travel time could translate into higher profits for the traders. Most of the emigrants, however, were primarily interested in getting to their destination. Any improvements on the trail were seen as a way of making their trip shorter. They were not concerned with improving the route to make it easier for strangers yet to come unless they could make some financial gain from it. The delay caused by building a raft to ferry others across for profit could be tolerated for a few days. Many of the improvements built along the Oregon and California Trails were later further improved or reconstructed by the military or government. They sometimes even surveyed and constructed new cutoffs or routes such as the Lander Road in 1859 and Captain Simpson's route across central Nevada.

By the mid-1840s the Santa Fe Trail was a well-established and well-known route. The main Oregon and California Trails had been developed and used by more than eight thousand emigrants. By 1846 California-bound emigrants had already pioneered a trail into the Great

Salt Lake Valley, crossed the Salt Lake Desert, and gone on to California. All this had happened before the Mormons entered the valley.

The years 1846 and 1847 saw the establishment of what is now called the Mormon Trail. The first segment of the Mormon Trail from Nauvoo, Illinois, to the Omaha, Nebraska, area was used in 1846. It was not over one of the other major established emigrant trails, but it did generally follow territorial roads and trading trails in Iowa. However, the second and major segment of the Mormon Trail, from the Winter Quarters in the Omaha area to the Valley of the Great Salt Lake was over much of the established route on the north side of the Platte River. It was previously used by many of the early trappers and emigrants to Oregon and California. As some historians have noted, with the exception of less than a mile at the mouth of Emigration Canyon in Utah, all of the main Mormon Trail was over the established routes of parts of the Oregon and California Trails.

While economic factors were largely responsible for the migration of emigrants over the Santa Fe, Oregon, and California Trails, religion was the primary reason for the migration of the Mormons along the trail. Many of the beliefs and ideas developed during the early years of the Mormon faith and church were different from the predominant religious views of citizens of that time. These differences led to strained relations with their non-Mormon, or Gentile, neighbors.

Not only do Mormons consider themselves to be Christians, they believe they are the "true" Christian Church, the original church established by Jesus Christ when he lived on the earth—"restored" to its rightful position—and that all present members are saints, "latter-day saints" as distinguished from the earlier saints. Because of this, they are often referred to as "the Saints." They believe that revelations from God continue in the present time. They hold that Joseph Smith, their founder, was a prophet who spoke with the inspiration and power of God as did the apostles and prophets of the Bible and as do their living prophets today. The Quorum of Twelve Apostles, the main governing body, had its basis in professed revelation, and its first members, including Brigham Young, were chosen for their steadfastness during the Zion Camp's March from Kirtland, Ohio, to Independence, Missouri, in 1834. The Quorum also has the power to speak with authority from God. In addition to the Bible, the Mormon scriptures include the Book of Mormon, which is claimed to be an ancient record of the early Americas; the Doctrine and Covenants, a collection of contemporary revelations, mostly to Joseph Smith; and the Pearl of Great Price, a collection of other writings and translations of Joseph Smith. These combined scriptures provide the basis for their faith and the guides for their behavior. Mormons also hold that they themselves are the children of Israel, the "chosen people."

Their organization, starting at the family level and continuing through to the highest positions in the church's organization is patriarchal. The father's authority over the family is considered supreme. All males twelve years and older who are considered worthy "hold the priesthood." In addition, there is a history of a strict giving, known as tithes and offerings, to the church and the belief that the commandments from God come first. However, the legitimate needs of the family, the basic unit of church organization, receive highest priority. Mormons feel that God did not prevent their suffering and persecution in order to test and refine them.

During much of the 19th century, they practiced polygamy as a revealed tenet of their faith. Many of these ideas and beliefs served to strengthen the church and build a strong Mormon discipline, but they also served to separate the Mormons from most other Americans. The theocratic nature of their political organization also conflicted with much of the popular political thinking at the time. All of these ideas and practices tended to separate the Mormons from others, and thus made them more susceptible to persecution. As religious persecution increased, the Mormons were forced to move from one place to another throughout the United States looking for a place to establish their Zion and live in peace.

The Mormons were first centered in New York, then they moved to Ohio and a variety of places in Missouri, and then to Nauvoo, Illinois. The Nauvoo site was selected by Joseph Smith in 1839. Originally it was only the tiny hamlet of Commerce. Much of the land surrounding it was miasmic marshlands that nobody wanted or thought could be used. Here Smith hoped that they could finally live in peace. Temporary structures may have been of logs, but the Mormons planned to stay. Nauvoo was built as a permanent center. The area was drained and the city was laid out in a grid pattern. Permanent structures were built. Homes and shops were constructed of brick. Education was considered important and a university was planned. A charter was obtained for the first city university in the country. The large temple structure of stone was built high on the hill overlooking the city and the Mississippi River. Nauvoo soon rivaled Chicago, Illinois, as the largest city in the state and became one of the twenty largest cities in the United States. But, as had happened in all the other places Mormons settled, persecution was soon to follow. Following the murder of Joseph Smith the Mormons were again driven out and forced to look for a new place to live and to practice their faith freely.

Thus, the reason for the Mormon migration was religious in motivation, and the migration itself was unlike most of the migrations of other emigrants traveling to Oregon and California. The Mormons had their migration forced upon them. For nearly two decades after their founding, the Mormons were forced from areas in which they lived. Later, many sought voluntarily to emigrate to Salt Lake City to live in their new Zion or Promised Land.

Another related facet of the Mormon migration that distinguished it from that of the other trails was the composition of the emigrants and their organization. It was noted earlier that most of the early American travelers on the Santa Fe Trail were males and relatively few women and children traveled on the trail. During the gold rush years those en route to California were also almost exclusively males. Even during the earlier years relatively few women traveled on that route. However, women, married and single, and children were more commonly found as members of companies on the Mormon Trail. Women and children often comprised the majority of the members of Mormon wagon companies. Only in the first Pioneer Company of 1847 was the population almost exclusively males. It was composed of 143 men (including three African Americans), 3 women, and 2 young boys. In addition, it should be noted that about 500 men had entered into military service and had formed the Mormon Battalion, which was sent south over the Santa Fe Trail to California during the Mexican War. The impact of both the Pioneer Company and the formation of the Mormon Battalion could explain why many of the later 1847 Mormon companies were composed mainly of women and children. However, an exodus of mostly women and children continued in later years.

Many of the non-Mormon, or Gentile, wagon companies were composed of a variety of people, including families, their relatives, and friends. Often members came from a particular area of the country. However, frequently there were also strangers who joined the company. Most companies were organized with both democratic and military elements. Leaders were chosen by the male members of the wagon company. All the members of the company were then expected to follow the orders of the captain. However, it seems that very few companies stayed together for the whole length of their journey or ended with the same officers as when they began. Records indicate that some companies started to break up within a few weeks. Emigrants frequently recorded in their diaries information about individual families that would drop out. Other diarists recorded how they picked up another wagon or family that had dropped out of a nearby company. Sometimes it was recorded that a lone wagon or family had been passed on the trail. It seems that the pressures of trail travel, the changes in their destination, or just the individualistic desires of these independent-minded emigrants brought a constant ebb and flow to wagon company membership. Sometimes harsh realities of disease or breakdowns forced members to fall behind and necessitated a change. The pressures of travel and the experience on the trail also caused companies to change their leadership. One of the rare companies that did not experience all this turmoil was the 1849 Washington City and California Mining Association company under the leadership of J. Goldsborough Bruff. Not until they were already in California and a few days from their goal did the company leave someone on the trail. It was their leader himself, J. Goldsborough Bruff, who had become too sick.

Mormon wagon companies, on the other hand, were much better organized. They often included large family groups and whole communities and generally remained together under the same leadership for the entire journey, helping each other all along the route. There were a number of factors that contributed to this. Within a few years after the development of the Mormon faith, its members tended to "gather" and to live in communities. However, as persecution increased, they tended to move into relatively unsettled areas where they established their own, separate communities. Because of increased persecutions, whole communities were forced to move. This was reflected in the main movement of Mormons from Kirtland, Ohio, to Jackson County, Missouri, in 1836, then to Far West, Missouri, in 1838, then in the Exodus from Nauvoo to Winter Quarters in 1846, and finally in 1847 when they moved from Winter Quarters to Salt Lake City.

Organization was not only a characteristic of travel in the United States. The Mormon immigrants from Europe usually came as an organized group on a chartered ship, then traveled together by train or riverboat to the jumping-off sites, and then finally migrated together in wagon or handcart companies to Salt Lake. Thus the Mormons traveled together in common groups with members who were well known to each other. Since there was a large number of people involved it was sometimes necessary to divide them into more than one wagon company, but even then the companies remained in close contact with one another. They were not a group of strangers who got together only for convenience, but rather they traveled with and remained together because they were organized to do so in order to help and support each other.

Some aspects of Mormon belief tended to result in much better organized companies. In January of 1847, Brigham Young, who was then head of the Mormon Church, received a revelation known as "The Word

SECTION CXXXVI

The Word and Will of the Lord, given through President Brigham Young, at the Winter Quarters of the Camp of Israel, Omaha Nation, West Bank of Missouri River, near Council Bluffs, January 14th, 1847.

1. The word and will of the Lord concerning the Camp of Israel in their journeyings to the West.

2. Let all the people of the Church of Jesus Christ of Latter-day Saints, and those who journey with them, be organized into companies, with a covenant and promises to keep all the commandments and statutes of the Lord our God.

3. Let the companies be organized with captains of hundreds, captains of fifties, and captains of tens, with a president and his two counselors at their heads, under the direction of the Twelve Apostles ;

4. All this shall be our covenant, that we will walk in all the ordinances of the Lord.

5. Let each company provide themselves with all the teams, wagons, provisions, clothing, and other necessa- ries for the journey that they can.

6. When the companies are organized, let them go to with their might, to prepare for those who are to tarry.

7. Let each company with their captains and presi- dents decided how many can go next spring ; then choose out a sufficient number of able-bodied and expert men, to take teams, seeds, and farming utensils, to go as pioneers to prepare for putting in spring crops.

8. Let each company bear an equal proportion, ac- cording to the dividend of their property, in tak- ing the poor, the widows, the fatherless, and the fami- lies of those who have gone into the army, that the cries of the widow and the fatherless come not up into the ears of the Lord against this people.

9. Let each company prepare houses and fields for raising grain, for those who are to remain behind this season, and this is the will of the Lord concerning his people.

10. Let every man use all his influence and prop- erty to remove this people to the place where the Lord shall locate a stake of Zion ;

11. And if ye do this with a pure heart, in all faith- fulness, ye shall be blessed ; you shall be blessed in your flocks, and in your herds, and in your fields, and in your houses, and in your families.

12. Let my servants Ezra T. Benson and Erastus Snow organize a company ; .

13. And let my servants Orson Pratt and Wilford Woodruff organize a company.

14. Also, let my servants Amasa Lyman and George A. Smith organize a company ;

15. And appoint presidents, and captains of hun- dreds, and of fifties, and of tens,

16. And let my servants that have been appointed go and teach this my will to the Saints, that they may be ready to go to a land of peace.

17. Go thy way and do as I have told you, and fear not thine enemies ; for they shall not have power to stop my works.

18. Zion shall be redeemed in mine own due time,

19. And if any man shall seek to build up himself, and seeketh not my council, he shall have no power, and his folly shall be made manifest.

20. Seek ye and keep all your pledges one with another, and covet not that which is thy brother's.

21. Keep yourselves from evil to take the name of the Lord in vain, for I am the Lord your God, even the God of your fathers, the God of Abraham, and of Isaac, and of Jacob.

22. I am he who led the children of Israel out of the land of Egypt, and my arm is stretched out in the last days to save my people Israel.

23. Cease to contend one with another, cease to speak evil one of another.

24. Cease drunkenness, and let your words tend to edifying one another.

25. If thou borrowest of thy neighbor, thou shalt return that which thou hast borrowed ; and if thou canst not repay, then go straight way and tell thy neighbor, lest he condemn thee.

26. If thou shalt find that which thy neighbor has lost, thou shalt make diligent search till thou shalt deliver it to him again.

27. Thou shalt be diligent in preserving what thou hast, that thou mayest be a wise steward ; for it is the free gift of the Lord thy God, and thou art his steward.

28. If thou art merry, praise the Lord with singing, with music, with dancing, and with a prayer of praise and thanksgiving.

29. If thou art sorrowful, call on the Lord thy God with supplication, that your soles may be joyful.

30. Fear not thine enemies, for they are in mine hands, and I will do my pleasure with them.

31. My people must be tried in all things, that they may be prepared to receive the glory that I have for them, even the glory of Zion, and he that will not bear chastisement, is not worthy of my kingdom.

32. Let him that is ignorant learn wisdom by humbling himself and calling upon the Lord his God, that his eyes may be opened that he may see, and his ears opened that he may hear.

33. For my spirit is sent forth into the world to enlighten the humble and contrite, and to the con- demna- tion of the ungodly.

34. Thy brethren have rejected you and your testi- mony, even the nation that has driven you out ;

35. And now cometh the day of their calamity, even the days of sorrow, like a woman that is taken in travail ; and their sorrow shall be great, unless they speedily repent ; yea, very speedily.

36. For they killed the Prophets, and them that were sent unto them, and they have shed innocent blood, which crieth from the ground against them :

37. Therefore marvel not at these things, for ye are not pure ; ye can not yet bear my glory ; but ye shall behold it if ye are faithful in keeping all my words that I have given you from the days of Adam to Abraham ; from Abraham to Moses ; from Moses to Jesus and his apostles ; and from Jesus and his apostles to Joseph Smith, whom I did call upon by mine angels, my ministering servants ; and by mine own voice out of the heavens to bring forth my work,

38. Which foundation he did lay, and was faithful and I took him to myself.

39. Many have marveled because of his death, but it was needful that he should seal his testimony with his blood, that he might be honored, and the wicked might be condemned.

40. Have I not delivered you from your enemies, only in that I have left a witness of my name?

41. Now, therefore, hearken, O ye people of my church ; and ye elders listen together ; you have receiv- ed my kingdom,

42. Be diligent in keeping all my commandments, lest judgements come upon you, and your faith fail you, and your enemies triumph over you.--So no more at present. Amen, and Amen.

THE END.

8

and Will of the Lord." One aspect of it included the plan of organization for migration to the West. This document is unique in the history of westward migration. It helps explain the success of the migration. The Mormon wagon company leaders were not democratically elected but were selected or appointed by church leaders. There were captains for the groups of wagons or families of hundreds, of fifties, and finally of tens. Because Mormons believed that their leaders spoke with authority from God, they were much less likely to question any of the orders or directions given by their leader or voice their disagreement with him. They also believed in the natural hierarchy of authority. Everyone was expected to follow those who had authority over them, and anyone below was expected to follow the directives of the leader above. Even the daily routine was prescribed. During the exodus from Nauvoo, Brigham Young set down the pattern which was followed. At five o'clock the bugle was sounded. People were awakened, prayers said, meals were cooked and eaten and teams were fed. At seven o'clock the bugle was sounded again and the wagon company was off. Each able-bodied man was assigned to his post, and he was not allowed to leave it without permission from the officers. There were rules for noon and evening stops. By eight thirty in the evening the bugle would sound again for evening prayers, and by nine o'clock the camp was to be at rest. It was also practice not to travel on Sundays. Gentile wagon companies sometimes followed this practice, but not as strongly as the Mormons did. Some historians hold that not traveling on Sunday for religious reasons had the added benefit of allowing both people and beasts to recuperate. This benefit may have actually offset any loss of travel time. Thus, the Mormon wagon companies and trains tended to run much more efficiently than the non-Mormon companies. Non-Mormon emigrants frequently commented in their diaries about the efficient organization and movement of the Mormon companies.

Another related difference concerns the professional organization and sponsorship of wagon companies. For the most part non-Mormon wagon companies were not professionally organized. Most organized themselves either at the jumping-off sites or after a few days out on the trail. There were only a limited number of attempts by professionals to organize companies which emigrants could join for a fee and where the business enterprise would provide the wagons, animals, supplies, etc. Most of these attempts failed because the companies were insufficiently supplied and lacked a sense of unity. The Pioneer Line was probably one of the most famous of these failures in its attempt to take emigrants quickly and safely to California in 1849.

As the number of Mormons wanting or needing to go to Salt Lake City grew, the Mormon Church became more involved in the development of the transportation systems to bring them to Salt Lake City. From the 1850s into the late 1860s the church sponsored three different systems to help Mormons migrate to Salt Lake. First was the establishment of the Perpetual Emigration Fund system. It was to help finance the migrations for those who could not afford it. Those emigrants who used the funds were expected to repay the system. Two systems were specifically developed to provide transportation for the emigrants to Salt Lake City. One was the "handcart system" developed in the mid-1850s, and the other involved the use of "down-and-back" wagon trains in the 1860s. Individual Mormons also provided considerable assistance in building the transcontinental railroad through Utah. The Golden Spike, which symbolized the completion of the transcontinental railroad by joining the tracks of the Union Pacific and Central Pacific railroads, was driven at Promontory Point, Utah, on May 10, 1869.

At the same time that the Mormons were converting new members in the United States, missionaries were sent across the seas to convert even more people. Another source of Mormon emigrants were the Mormon converts from Europe. As early as 1842 church leaders such as Brigham Young were sent to Europe as missionaries. By the mid-1850s thousands of converts came to the United States from a variety of European countries. The British Isles and the Scandinavian countries provided the largest number of converts, but others came from France, Germany, Switzerland, Spain, and Italy. The Mormons were also active in South America, South Africa, and the South Seas. After the converts arrived, those going west migrated along the Mormon Trail to the Valley of the Great Salt Lake, while those from the Pacific coast traveled east into the valley. From there they spread throughout Utah, Arizona, Idaho, Nevada, and even into California.

Thousands had been converted in Europe, and this resulted in a problem of transporting them safely across the sea and then to Salt Lake City. The establishment of the Perpetual Emigration Fund in 1850 helped to solve this problem. It was established "to promote, facilitate, and accomplish the Emigration of the Poor." In typical Mormon fashion, much planning and organization went into the program. Once the fund was established, it was intended to be self-sustaining. Emigrants could borrow from the fund to help pay for passage to the United States and then for their journey to Salt Lake itself. It was expected that the emigrants making use of the fund would repay it after they became established. As is often the case with programs such as this, the monies were not always repaid. However, the Church continued to support the program with funds raised by the tithes of all Mormons. Mormon agents would contract for the use of a ship, provide for food on the journey, and then arrange transportation by rail or ship to the jumping-off sites of the Mormon Trail. By 1887, when the program ceased, perhaps as many as 100,000 Mormons had been assisted on their journey to Zion. Later converts arrived in Salt Lake on the transcontinental railroad.

One of the truly unique features of the Mormon Trail was the development and use of handcart companies, which, for a few years, supplemented the use of wagons. The wagon was the usual method of transportation employed by both Mormons and non-Mormons alike on the trails. The emigrant wagon was not the large Conestoga wagon used back east on the National Road or similar wagons sometimes employed by traders on the Santa Fe Trail, but was typically a small farm wagon about eight to ten feet long and usually between thirty-eight to forty-two inches wide. It might be pulled by oxen, mules, or horses. Emigrants often argued amongst themselves about the advantages of each type of team. Oxen were usually stronger, slower, cheaper, and could eat a wider variety of vegetation and, thus, could subsist better along the trail. They were also a little less likely to be stolen. Mules were less expensive than horses but more expensive than oxen, but they could travel faster than oxen. Horses were the fastest, the most expensive, and had feed requirements that were the hardest to provide for during the early years of trail travel. They were also the most likely to be stolen by the Indians. Although all draft animals were used by Mormons, it seems that oxen were employed most often.

There are a few examples of the use of carts by non-Mormons on the emigrant trails. At first people did not even think that wagons could be taken west over the Oregon and California Trails. Some of the early trading companies used carts and wagons to bring supplies out to the early mountain men rendezvous in the Rocky Mountains. But none of these were handcarts and none had ever taken them all the way over the mountains. One of the first attempts to bring an emigrant wagon west actually ended with the wagon being cut in two and being used as a cart to finally complete the journey to Oregon. This was the case in 1836 when the missionaries Marcus and Narcissa Whitman went west. At Fort Hall they were forced to cut their wagon and to continue to Oregon with it as a cart. Carts were associated with two other areas. One area was in the Red River Valley of the Dakotas and Minnesota. Carts were also used in the Southwest by the native Mexicans. However, it was the Mormons who perfected the system of handcart companies for the mass movement of people and goods west.

In the 1850s Iowa City, Iowa, was located near the western terminus of the eastern railroad. Mormons from Europe and the East came west to Iowa by train. The handcart companies were developed to bring the Mormons from the end of the railroad to Salt Lake City. The Mormon Church financed the construction of the handcarts and their use. While there seem to have been different sizes of handcarts, the typical cart had a bed approximately three feet wide, four feet long, and nine inches deep. The wheels were four feet in diameter with ten spokes. They were much cheaper to build than wagons, but they also only carried about 500 lbs, much less than wagons. This necessitated re-supply locations, or way-stations, along the trail. The carts were harder on the emigrants because draft animals were usually not used to pull them. The emigrants them-selves provided the power to pull or push them. From 1856 until 1860 ten handcart companies carried about three thousand Mormons to Salt Lake City. Generally they traveled faster than wagon companies and were considered to be a success. Many people, however, only remember the stories of the Martin and Willie Handcart Companies that got caught in blizzards in Wyoming in 1856. They suffered great loss of life and became the worst recorded disasters on the emigrant trails during the period of westward migration. It should also be noted that when individ-ual Mormons were given a chance to select their method of transporta-tion and could afford it, the wagon was preferred over the handcart.

From 1860 until 1868 the church was involved in providing the physical wagons, stock, and supplies necessary for emigration to Salt Lake City. These could be considered to be professional companies. They were known as "down-and-back" companies or wagon trains. They were organized in Salt Lake City to go back and forth between Salt Lake City and the jumping-off cities. Geographically, the church was subdivided into stakes and wards, each with their own officers. In its early period, the local level of organization, or ward, usually consisted of between 200 to 1,200 people. Approximately ten wards were combined to form a stake. Under the leadership of Brigham Young and the church, all Mor-mon wards were required to provide wagons, draft animals, supplies, drivers, and other equipment necessary for a possible six-month trip. Thus, the wagon train only had to pick up the emigrants at the jumping-off sites. The emigrants did not have to purchase their wagons, etc. All the "down-and-back" wagon companies successfully made the journey to Salt Lake City. The first four church companies of 1861 included 203 wagons, 235 teamsters and guards, and 1,699 oxen with 136,000 pounds of flour. During this whole period more than 2,000 wagons with 2,500 teamsters brought over 20,000 emigrants to Salt Lake City. With the completion of the railroad in 1869 the church no longer had to organize wagon companies to bring Mormon emigrants into Utah.

Another way in which the Mormon's highly organized nature was reflected was in their desire to make the trip for subsequent Mormons easier. They established communities and made improvements along their route. This was first done during their exodus from Nauvoo. They knew that it would not be possible to evacuate everyone at once. In Iowa, three centers, or way stations, were established along the route to their Winter Quarters area. They were Garden Grove, Mount Pisgah, and the Kanesville camp, which became present-day Council Bluffs. These camps, located in Iowa, were not temporary camps. At Mount Pisgah, shelters were built, fields were cleared and fenced, crops were planted, a mill was built, and a tabernacle was constructed. Similar locations were established along the trail to Salt Lake City. Fort Supply was built near Fort Bridger in Wyoming. One of its functions was to aid the Mormon emigrants by providing supplies to those coming across the plains. In 1861 four camps were established by the "down-and-back" wagon companies. Three were in Wyoming at Rocky Ridge, North Platte Bridge, and Deer Creek, and one was located in Nebraska at Wood River. This practice was continued in other parts of the United States as the Mormons spread out from Salt Lake City to surrounding areas.

Crossing rivers was a major obstacle for all emigrants. For the rivers that were too deep to ford, ferries were used. The Mormons built a number of ferries along their route. They established three ferries over the Missouri River in the Kanesville or Omaha area. Perhaps the most famous of the ferries was the Mormon Ferry at present-day Casper, Wyoming. Another important ferry was established further southwest on the Green River. The ferries served two purposes. One was to ensure safe passage for the Mormon emigrants, and the second, by charging a fee, was to provide additional funds to the Mormon Church in an area where cash was hard to come by. All along the route to Salt Lake City, Mormons made improvements on the established trails by building ferries, clearing the trails, putting up mileage signs, and establishing communities to provide shelter and supplies for the later migrating Mormons.

Thus, one can see how a variety of factors combined with the practices of the Mormon faith and church made the Mormon Trail unique in the history of westward migrations.

JAMES & MARGARET REED—California
Department of Parks and Recreation

James and Margaret Reed were members of the 1846 Donner-Reed Party. They had heard about Hastings's new cutoff to California. At Fort Bridger the party turned off the established trail. They had already fallen behind the main companies but hoped they could catch up to those companies which were being guided by Hastings. When the Donner-Reed Party arrived at the Weber River, they met Hastings. Hastings suggested that the Donner-Reed Party take a different route which he said would be easier than the difficult route down the Weber River that he used to take the earlier parties. The new route was over the Wasatch Mountains. It turned out to be much worse than the river route. The Donner-Reed Party had to cut the route over the mountains. This was an extremely difficult task that further slowed their party's progress. Because of the loss of time there and later on the trail to California, they were ultimately caught in a snowstorm and were forced to stay the winter on the east side of the Sierras. The rest of their terrible ordeal is well known. Their contribution to the development of the Mormon Trail was their cutting of the section of trail over the Wasatch and down Emigration Canyon into the valley that the Mormon pioneer vanguard party followed in 1847.

PART I

Early History

JOSEPH SMITH—Library of Congress

Joseph Smith was the prophet and organizer of the Church of Jesus Christ of Latter-day Saints, or Mormon Church. When Joseph Smith was a young boy he had a religious vision. That vision and others ultimately led to the discovery and translation of the golden plates into the Book of Mormon. Within a short time he formed the Mormon Church. The early years of the Church brought increasing persecution of himself and of other Mormons. Moving from New York to Ohio, to Missouri, and then to Illinois, he was constantly trying to find a safe place for the "Saints." In 1839, he moved the center of Mormonism to Nauvoo, Illinois, but within a short time, persecution occurred even there. For Joseph Smith, finding a peaceful spot for the Mormons to live proved to be elusive. In 1844, Joseph Smith and his brother Hyrum Smith were killed by an angry mob.

The Mormon Church, the Development of the Mormon Trail, and Mormon Migrations: 1803–1869

UNLIKE THE HISTORY OF THE OREGON, CALIFORNIA, AND SANTA FE Trails, the history and development of the Mormon Trail is a story of both the usage and improvement of previously identified routes and of the religious events that influenced the migration of Mormons west to Utah and the Great Basin.

1803

President Thomas Jefferson purchased a vast tract of land west of the Mississippi River from the French government. This was the single largest peaceful expansion of the United States in its history. The lands included in the Louisiana Purchase contained most of the area through which the Mormons would later pass. However, the territory of Utah and the Valley of the Great Salt Lake, the future site of their new Zion, were not included in the purchase. They were located in Mexican territory.

1804–1806

The exploration of the newly purchased Louisiana Territory was con- ducted by Meriwether Lewis and William Clark. The route they used in their westward journey of exploration was centered in the northern part of the territory along the Missouri River Valley and into the area along the Pacific Coast west of the Rocky Mountains jointly claimed by the United States and Great Britain and commonly known as Oregon. It was the interest in the Oregon Territory and the fantastic stories of those areas that ultimately resulted in the development of trapper and emigrant routes that the Mormons would later follow and improve.

1805

The Prophet Joseph Smith was born on December 23 near Sharon, Vermont. He spent the first ten years of his life in a variety of places in or near the Green Mountains of New England. In 1816 his family moved to New York. Two other individuals, Brigham Young and Heber Kimball, were born in New England in 1801. All these men later played crucial leadership roles in the Mormon religion.

1812–13

John Jacob Astor tried to expand his fur trading empire into the Oregon Territory. Although this attempt did not succeed, knowledge about the route west grew. A returning party of his "Astorians," led by Robert Stuart, learned of the South Pass. However, because of Indians in the area at that time, the pass was not used. It took another twelve years before it was.

1820

According to the accepted account, at age fourteen, Joseph had his First Vision of the Father and the Son in a grove of trees by his home near Manchester, New York. This was the beginning of his religious awakening and what, within the Mormon Church, is also considered to be the beginning of the restoration of the original Church of Jesus Christ, which he established when he lived upon the earth. Later, the angel Moroni visited Joseph and showed him where the golden plates were buried.

1820s

During the next two decades the importance of fur trapping grew in the Rocky Mountains. Trappers and traders increased their knowledge of the lands in the Rockies and of the route from the Mississippi/Missouri rivers along the Platte River Valley. By the 1830s traffic increased along the river systems and general routes west were established.

1824

William Henry Ashley began the practice of conducting a rendezvous. Most of the well-known mountain men were getting their start in the fur business. Men such as Jim Bridger, James Clyman, Joseph Reddeford Walker, Jedediah Smith, Thomas Fitzpatrick, and others were developing survival skills and learning about the area from the Mississippi/Missouri

Valley to the Rockies. Most of these mountain men later became associated with the development of the Santa Fe, Oregon, and California Trails. Some of them also came to be associated with sites and events on the Mormon Trail.

South Pass was rediscovered by trappers, and it became the regular route through the Rocky Mountains. Jedediah Smith, William Sublette, and James Clyman are believed to be some of the first to actually use the route.

Independence Rock was given its name as a result of visiting trappers, including Tom Fitzpatrick, who camped and celebrated Independence Day there. Some historians believe William Sublette named the rock in 1830. In 1841 Pierre DeSmet gave Independence Rock its name as the "Register of the Desert" because of the practice of passing emigrants and trappers who wrote or carved their names on the rock.

Jim Bridger was reported to have discovered the Great Salt Lake as a result of a bet with other trappers about the course of the Bear River. He supposedly floated down the river in a "bull boat" made of buffalo skins and entered the Great Salt Lake.

1827

Joseph Smith began the translation of the golden plates into the Book of Mormon. It was finally finished in 1830. The Book of Mormon, called another testament of Jesus Christ, purports to be the history of God's dealings with the inhabitants of the Western Hemisphere who were descendants of Joseph of the Bible.

Independence, Missouri, was established. The area soon became the major outfitting area for the Santa Fe Trail and by the 1840s was a major jumping-off site for the Oregon-and California-bound emigrants. Later some Mormon wagon companies also used the area.

1828

Hiram Scott, a trapper, was left for dead by his companions. In 1829 William Sublette found a skeleton believed to be Scott's. The large bluffs near where the bones were found were named after him. Scotts Bluff then served as a landmark along the Platte River and the emigrant trails in the area.

1830

On April 6, Joseph Smith, along with five others, and (as they testified) under the direction of Jesus Christ, organized the Church of Christ, which, eight years later, became the Church of Jesus Christ of Latter-day

Saints (Mormon), in Fayette/Colesville, New York. This is also the site of his first arrest and persecution for his religious beliefs.

1831

In January Joseph Smith received a revelation to move the church to Kirtland, Ohio. Smith started an extensive building program. Laying out broad streets on strict compass settings with large city lots, he transformed the small city to a center of Mormonism with its own temple. Later, in July, while visiting Independence, Missouri, he also received another revelation that Independence, Missouri, be designated as "the land of promise, and the place for the city of Zion." Both areas served as centers for the Mormon Church from 1831–1837. Today, Independence is the headquarters of the Reorganized Church of Jesus Christ of Latter Day Saints.

1832–35

Captain Benjamin L. E. Bonneville, on a leave of absence from the military, led an expedition west to the Rocky Mountains. He hired Joseph Reddeford Walker, who explored a route to California and the region around the Great Salt Lake. In 1837 Washington Irving published Bonneville's journals and maps, *The Adventures of Captain Bonneville in the Rocky Mountains and the Far West*. The book was very popular and sparked interest in the area.

1833–38

In Missouri relations with non-Mormons deteriorated, forcing the Mormons to move around from place to place. The problem culminated when the Missouri government set forth its infamous "Extermination Order," which stated that the Mormons must be expelled or exterminated.

1834

Fort William was built near the mouth of the Laramie River where it meets the Platte River. Robert Campbell built the log fort. It was named for his partner, William Sublette, but the fort is commonly called Fort Laramie. This wooden structure was immortalized by Alfred J. Miller in 1837, when Sir William Drummond Stewart brought him along on his tour of the west to record in paintings his trip. The fort changed hands a number of times and was replaced with an adobe fort in 1841.

1836

The Mormon settlement of Far West was established in northern Missouri. It briefly served as a major center for the Mormons.

1837–41

Father Pierre Jean DeSmet helped establish a mission in the area known as Council Bluffs. Father DeSmet became one of the most famous, knowledgeable, and influential people of the West. He traveled back and forth from the Council Bluffs area to the west along what became a well-established route. His counsel was sought by emigrants and the government when dealing with Indians. Council Bluffs became one of the jumping-off places for the migrations west and was also known as Kanesville when the Mormons occupied the area (1846–1852).

1838

In Ohio, relations with non-Mormons also worsened. On July 6, Joseph Smith was finally forced to move his followers in 58 wagons with 515 people west out of Ohio to the town/site of Far West, Missouri.

Missouri Governor Lilburn W. Boggs issued the infamous order which called for the Mormons to be "exterminated or driven from the state if necessary for public peace."

As conditions in Missouri continued to deteriorate, rumors spread and conflict erupted into fighting at the Battle of Crooked River in October, and then again at Haun's Mill. Shortly thereafter, Joseph and his brother Hyrum Smith and several other Mormon leaders who did not participate in the battle surrendered to the authorities and were imprisoned at Liberty Jail. The rest of the Mormons were able to escape to Far West. Joseph and Hyrum Smith later escaped, too. They were forced once again to look for a new home, this time in Illinois.

1839

Joseph Smith selected the site of a small, nearly forgotten hamlet of Commerce for the city of Zion, which he called "Nauvoo." Nauvoo (claimed by Smith to come from a Hebrew word meaning "a beautiful plantation or place") became the center of the Mormon Church. Within five years it had a population of nearly 20,000 and was one of the largest cities in the United States. The city and the Mormons received a special charter from the state legislature. Nauvoo was granted autonomy over a number of governmental functions, including taxes and courts, and it was even given the right to maintain its own independent militia, known as the Nauvoo Legion. It was here that the Nauvoo Temple was built. After the murder of Joseph and Hyrum Smith, and increased religious persecution, the Mormon exodus from Nauvoo began in 1846. Nauvoo is considered to be the beginning site of the Mormon Pioneer Trail.

1841

The old wooden Fort William on the Laramie River was replaced by the adobe fort called Fort John. However, like its predecessor, Fort John was also commonly called Fort Laramie. It is this Fort Laramie that was visited by the Mormon pioneers. The fort marks the place in the trail where the Mormons and other emigrants traveling on the north side of the Platte River forded to the south side and picked up the main Oregon Trail and followed it to Fort Bridger. It is also located at what is considered to be the western edge of the plains where the climb into the mountains commences.

The Bidwell-Bartleson Party, the first emigrant wagon company, left the Independence, Missouri, area for Oregon and California. They followed the main Oregon Trail until the party split into two groups at Sheep Rock near Soda Springs, Idaho. Father DeSmet, Thomas Fitzpatrick, and Joseph Meek served as their guides for part of the journey. One group headed for California and the other continued on to Oregon. The California-bound emigrants, the Bidwell-Bartleson Party, followed the Bear River south until it reached the Great Salt Lake, then they headed west around the north side of the lake, and finally south. They were forced to abandon some wagons in Utah and their remaining ones in Nevada, then continue by horseback into California. They were the first wagon company to traverse the area that later became the state of Utah.

1842–45

Captain John Charles Frémont left from Independence to explore the region to the South Pass and the Rocky (Wind River) Mountains. Charles Preuss served as his cartographer. Their work during this expedition and subsequent expeditions resulted in the publication of Frémont's reports to Congress and the publication of his large map showing the areas he explored. In 1843 Frémont explored the Great Salt Lake region. The areas shown on his maps include the land from Independence to Oregon and parts of California and back through Salt Lake Valley. It was these maps that Brigham Young and other Mormons had with them in 1847 when they left their Winter Quarters. (See also the map section for reproductions of some of the Frémont maps.)

1842

Emigrant wagon companies continued to head for Oregon. The general wagon route was becoming established. With the subsequent publication of Frémont's first map showing the route to the South Pass, emigrants were more confident about their journey west.

Dr. Elijah White led a wagon company to Oregon. Lansford Hastings was a member of this group. He later wrote his infamous guidebook to Oregon and California, in which he proposed his cutoff route to California by heading southwest from Fort Bridger and across the Great Salt Lake Desert.

1842–43

Jim Bridger and his partner Louis Vasquez built a trading post near the Black's Fork of the Green River. This site is where the Hastings Cutoff left the established Oregon-California Trail and headed southwest over the Wasatch Mountains to enter the Valley of the Great Salt Lake. The Mormons later purchased Fort Bridger and strengthened its fortification by building a stone fort.

1844

Relations between the Mormons and non-Mormons continued to worsen in Missouri and Illinois. On June 27 Joseph Smith and his brother Hyrum were killed. They were in the Carthage Jail awaiting trial when a mob stormed the jail and shot them.

Brigham Young, as President of the Quorum of Twelve Apostles, was sustained as leader of the Mormon Church.

1845

Under increasing pressure from the Gentiles and concern for the safety of the Mormons, Brigham Young agreed to leave Illinois "as soon as the grass grows and the water runs."

Lansford Hastings's guidebook, *The Emigrants' Guide to Oregon and California*, was published. It extolled the virtues of his cutoff to California. Mormon leaders read John Frémont's reports of his 1842 and 1843–44 explorations, Hastings's guide, and the earlier reports of Charles Wilkes and Benjamin Bonneville giving them much of the most recent information available about the West.

1846

Increases in persecution forced an early exodus from Nauvoo. On February 4, the first Mormons were ferried across the Mississippi River to Montrose, Iowa, from where they traveled to Sugar Creek. Then, for a short time, the river froze over completely, making the passage out of Nauvoo easier. The exodus from Nauvoo across Iowa to Council Bluffs and across

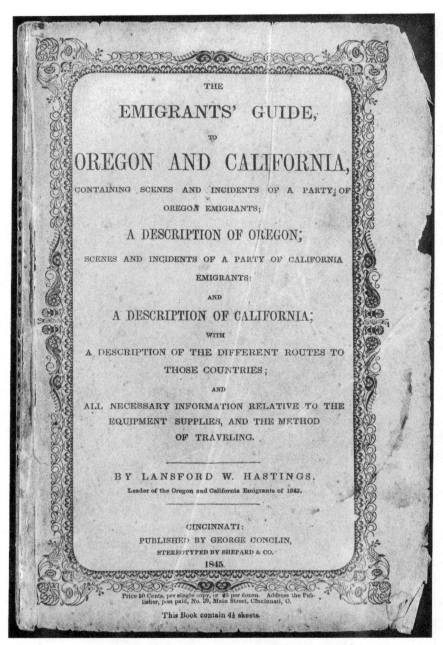

THE

EMIGRANTS' GUIDE,

TO

OREGON AND CALIFORNIA,

CONTAINING SCENES AND INCIDENTS OF A PARTY OF
OREGON EMIGRANTS;

A DESCRIPTION OF OREGON;

SCENES AND INCIDENTS OF A PARTY OF CALIFORNIA
EMIGRANTS:

AND

A DESCRIPTION OF CALIFORNIA;

WITH

A DESCRIPTION OF THE DIFFERENT ROUTES TO
THOSE COUNTRIES;

AND

ALL NECESSARY INFORMATION RELATIVE TO THE
EQUIPMENT SUPPLIES, AND THE METHOD
OF TRAVELING.

BY LANSFORD W. HASTINGS.

Leader of the Oregon and California Emigrants of 1842.

CINCINNATI:
PUBLISHED BY GEORGE CONCLIN,
STEREOTYPED BY SHEPARD & CO.
1845.

Price 50 Cents, per single copy, or $5 per dozen. Address the Pub-
lisher, post paid, No. 39, Main Street, Cincinnati, O.

This Book contain 4½ sheets.

**THE COVER OF HASTINGS'S *THE EMIGRANTS'
GUIDE TO OREGON AND CALIFORNIA***

the Missouri River to Winter Quarters represented the first stage of the Mormons' westward migration to their New Zion. The first group of Mormons under Brigham Young arrived on the Missouri River on June 5. On June 22, the first large group of wagons reached Council Bluffs, first called Miller's Hollow by the Mormons. The first segment of the Mormon Trail was now established. Consideration was being given to both California and the area of the Great Salt Lake as possible sites for their New Zion. Both were located on Mexican lands. Initially Young had planned to cover the distance from Nauvoo to the Rocky Mountains in one trip. However, it soon became apparent that that would be impossible. Through negotiations with both the government of the Territory of Iowa and the Pottawattamie and Omaha Indians, Brigham Young obtained permission to allow the Mormons to establish camps on Indian lands.

William Clayton wrote the famous Mormon hymn "Come, Come, Ye Saints." This hymn symbolizes both the Mormons' hardships and their strengths.

Winter Quarters was established on the west bank of the Missouri River in Omaha Indian Territory. A town was laid out for approximately three to four thousand Saints in what is now Florence, a suburb of Omaha. Other Saints were strung out across Iowa in the way-stations such as Garden Grove and Mount Pisgah. The journey across Iowa was extremely difficult and the winter of 1846–47 was also very hard on the Mormons. Many died on their journey and more died during that terrible winter.

War with Mexico was declared. Areas in contention included what are now California, Nevada, Utah, Arizona, New Mexico, and parts of Colorado and Wyoming.

Fighting continued to occur in Nauvoo. The last major group of Mormons was driven out in September.

The Mormon Battalion was formed by Mormons camped in the Kanesville area. Five hundred Mormons agreed to serve in the U.S. Army in the war against Mexico. They reported to Fort Leavenworth and then left from there for Mexico and California by way of the Santa Fe Trail. By agreement, much of the money paid to the battalion for a clothing allowance was given to the Mormon Church. It was then used to help finance the journey west for the rest of the Mormons to their new Zion in Utah. Many of the individuals who joined later played significant roles in the discovery of gold in California, in the opening of the Carson route on the California Trail, and in the development of Hensley's Salt Lake Cutoff north around the Great Salt Lake as another of the routes associated with the California Trail system.

The Donner-Reed party following Hastings's guidebook and advice headed southwest from Fort Bridger over the Hastings Cutoff. The route they used to cut over the Wasatch Mountains was later used by the Mormons' Pioneer Company in 1847. Their route became the last segment of the Mormon Trail to Salt Lake. Partially because of the delays caused in cutting the wagon route over the Wasatch, the Donner-Reed Party reached the Sierra Nevada late in the fall and were snowed in on the east side of the mountains. The story of that terrible winter and the death and devastation they faced is well documented in other books.

1847

The second phase in the development of the Mormon Trail began. There were to be two groups: first, a small exploring party, and then, the larger body of the Saints. On April 5, the vanguard party of the Mormons' Pioneer Company moved out of Winter Quarters. On June 21, east of Fort Bridger, Brigham Young and Jim Bridger discussed the nature of the area surrounding the Great Salt Lake. Brigham Young's journal records that Bridger stated that he would give one thousand dollars for the first bushel of corn grown in the Salt Lake Valley. On July 22, the exploring party of the Mormon Pioneers broke through the last major obstacle in Emigration Canyon and entered the Valley of the Great Salt Lake. On the 24th, Young's company came in full view of the Great Salt Lake. According to tradition, Brigham Young is reported to have declared, "This is the right place, move on!" and the second stage of the Mormon exodus from Nauvoo was completed. Thereafter, July 24 was celebrated by the Mormons as Pioneer Day. To this day, it is a state holiday in Utah.

The Mormons laid out Great Salt Lake City under Brigham Young's direction. Streets were built along a north-south grid and were wide enough for a wagon and team to turn around. New arrivals needing work were assigned to help build walls in and around the city. Camping areas in the city were set aside for newly arrived emigrants. Within a few years Salt Lake City, which had been the end of the Mormon Trail, developed into the hub, or crossroads, for the Great Basin. Major trails to California and throughout the Great Basin passed through or originated in Salt Lake City. The Hastings Cutoff continued west; Hensley's, or the Salt Lake, Cutoff headed north, and a connecting trail led southwest to join the Old Spanish Trail which went to southern California. These helped Salt Lake City to develop into an economic and social center in the West. Later, Benjamin Ferris, secretary of Utah Territory, called Salt Lake City the "half-way house between the eastern and western portions of the continent."

STONE WALLS-Today

This picture shows some of the original cobble-stone walls that newly arriving Saints helped to build. These old walls are being incorporated into a new wall in a new park by Temple Square.

1848

War with Mexico was formally over. The Treaty of Guadalupe Hidalgo was signed. Utah was no longer part of Mexico but now part of the United States.

Samuel J. Hensley opened the Salt Lake Cutoff of the California Trail from Salt Lake to City of Rocks in present-day southern Idaho. The route was first opened to wagons by a party of Mormon Battalion veterans traveling east to Utah from California.

According to legend, seagulls saved the crops by descending upon the fields near Salt Lake City and consuming the grasshoppers, or Mormon locusts, that had been eating the plants.

1849

The California Gold Rush started. Thousands of gold seekers flooded into Utah and Salt Lake City during the next few years on their way to the California gold fields. Once again relations between Mormons and Gentiles were sometimes tested. The influx of the argonauts, or gold seekers, increased the demand on the Mormons' limited food and supplies. However, the sale of supplies and provisions brought in needed cash for the Mormons.

The Mormons organized the Provisional State of Deseret (honey bee) with Brigham Young as its governor. The area in the original petition to Congress was comprised of the Great Basin area, including Utah, Nevada, parts of Idaho, Oregon, Wyoming, New Mexico, Arizona, and a portion of southern California to the seacoast near San Diego.

1849–52

Kanesville, Iowa, became the major jumping-off place for the Mormon migrations during this period.

1850

The Provisional State of Deseret was broken up. The area was established as a United States Territory and was divided as part of the Compromise of 1850. Utah is a much smaller area than Deseret was. Brigham Young became the first Utah territorial governor.

The Golden Pass Road was opened up on July 4th as a toll road to bring emigrants into Salt Lake City. Parley Pratt had started exploring for a new route in 1848. At the junction of Echo and Weber canyons the new route turns south up the Weber River and then over to and down Parley's Canyon to Salt Lake City. The following year traffic over the new route was down. A number of factors caused this decline: Pratt sold the toll road to help finance his mission work; the new route was longer than the old route; the old route was free; and costs for its upkeep were high. The new route fell into disuse for a short time. However, by the early to mid–1860s, with its constant improvements, Parley's route finally replaced the old trail that had entered through Emigration Canyon as the main route into Salt Lake City. Today I–80 generally follows the Golden Pass Road's route.

The Mormon Church established its Perpetual Emigration Fund to help finance or provide loans to poor Mormons facilitating their migration to Salt Lake Valley. The success of this fund helped to bring thousands of Mormons to Salt Lake City who would not otherwise have been able to afford the journey, especially those new converts from Europe. The fund was finally abolished in 1887.

1853

Keokuk, Iowa, became the main jumping-off point for the Mormons.

Construction on the Mormon Temple in Salt Lake City began. It was completed and dedicated in 1893—forty years later.

Fort Supply was established for a variety of reasons by the Mormons a few miles southwest of Fort Bridger: It helped to extend Mormon influence into the Green River area; it provided a base for missionary functions to the Indians; and it was a means to control the ferries in the Green River area. Fort Supply served as another Mormon colony to grow food and to provide help and protection for the Mormon emigrants. This was evident during the time of the two handcart disasters of 1856. It could also serve as a first line of defense for Salt Lake City against future persecutors. In order to consolidate forces Brigham Young later ordered Fort Supply and Fort Bridger burned when fear grew about hostilities with the United States that had developed during the Utah War.

1854

Westport, Missouri, near Independence, served as the main outfitting site for Mormons who would follow the route often considered to be the Oregon Trail.

1855

Mormon Grove, near Atchinson, Kansas, became the jumping-off area for Mormon departures. Mormons purchased Fort Bridger and strengthened its defenses by constructing stone walls.

1856–58

Iowa City, Iowa, became the major outfitting point for Mormon emigrants bound for Salt Lake City. Iowa City was across the river from the western end of the railroad.

1856–60

A new method of transporting Mormon immigrants to Salt Lake City was developed. Handcarts were built and provided for newly arriving immigrants to use on their journey to Salt Lake City. During this period, ten handcart companies took about 3,000 Saints to Salt Lake City. Iowa City served as the starting point of the Mormon Trail. Most of the Mormon converts traveled by rail to Iowa City. The handcart journey began there.

Two major handcart disasters happened in 1856. Both companies got late starts, and both were hit by early and constantly stormy winter weather. Late in October, Captain James G. Willie's company was caught in a blizzard east of the South Pass. Seventy-seven members out of 404 died. Then, in November, 576 members of Handcart Company No. 4, led by Captain Edward Martin, were trapped by a blizzard a few miles west of Devil's Gate. By the time they were rescued, 145 members had died.

These were the worst disasters during the migration of 1841–69. The total loss of life experienced because of these two disasters was much worse than that experienced by the members of the Donner Party who lost 40 members after they were caught in the snow in the Sierras in 1846.

1857–59

The so-called Mormon or Utah War caused tremendous strain between the Mormons and the Gentiles. President Buchanan replaced Brigham Young with Alfred Cumming as territorial governor and sent the U.S. Army, under command of Colonel Albert Sidney Johnston, into Utah to put down the so-called Mormon rebellion. With minor exceptions of harrassment (driving off horses and cattle, burning feed, grass, and wagons, etc.) there was no major fighting between the Mormons and the U.S. Army. It was during this time that the Mormons burned Fort Supply and Fort Bridger. The U.S. Army took over Fort Bridger and rebuilt it. Later the army established Camp Floyd 40 miles south of Salt Lake City. Thomas Kane, a man respected by the Mormons and the U.S. government helped to bring about a peaceful resolution of the problems.

1859–63

Florence, Nebraska, site of the 1846 Winter Quarters, once again became the main outfitting area for Mormon emigrant companies.

1860–61

The Pony Express was established. Part of its route was along portions of the Mormon, Oregon, and California Trails.

1861

The Church established the use of "down-and-back" wagon trains to transport Mormons from the jumping-off towns along the Missouri River to Salt Lake City. Each ward of the Mormon Church was given the responsibility of providing wagons, teams, supplies, and/or drivers. Four wagon companies started east on April 23 to pick up the first Mormons at Florence, Nebraska. The first church sponsored wagon company departed Florence on May 29 and arrived in Salt Lake on August 16. For the next few years this church supported endeavor helped to bring thousands of Mormons to Utah who might not have been able to do so on their own.

1864–66

The village of Wyoming, Nebraska, on the west bank of the Missouri River, northwest of Nebraska City, became the jumping-off place for the

MORMON CAMP AT WYOMING, NEBRASKA—
Savage, Nebraska State Historical Society

This picture by Charles Savage shows a Mormon encampment at Wyoming, Nebraska, in 1866. This was one jumping-off site used by the Mormons during the years 1864–66.

1,000 MILE TREE—Jackson, National Park Service

Jackson photographed the construction of the railroad west during 1869. Here is a later painting showing the railroad through Weber Canyon, 1,000 miles west of Omaha. Once the transcontinental railroad was completed, emigrants could travel west much faster and more easily. Subsequently, all the western trails fell into disuse.

Mormon migrations. The "down-and-back" wagon companies picked up the emigrants and brought them to Salt Lake City.

1867

The Mormon Tabernacle in Salt Lake City, with its huge elliptical dome, was completed.

By then the Union Pacific Railroad had already crossed the Missouri River. The terminus was North Platte, Nebraska. Mormons took the railroad to there and then started their wagon trips west. By 1868 the railroad was in Laramie, Wyoming, and later that summer in Benton. Both towns briefly served as wagon outfitting areas.

1869

The Union Pacific Railroad completed laying track and joined the Central Pacific at Promontory Summit on May 10. Mormons could now travel by rail to Utah. The railroad replaced the Mormon Trail, which had served them so faithfully.

PART II

Maps, Guidebooks, and Diaries

LANSFORD HASTINGS—The Bancroft Library

Lansford Hastings was an early pioneer to Oregon and California. He dreamed of creating his own empire in California. His primary contribution to the development of the Mormon Trail was the publishing of his emigrant guide which proposed a new purportedly shorter route to California, the Hastings Cutoff. It recommended leaving the main trail at Fort Bridger and heading southwest. In 1846 he met some emigrants going to California and persuaded them to use his new route. While he safely guided most parties over his new route, one was not as fortunate. The route from Fort Bridger southwest to the Valley of the Great Salt Lake was incorporated into the Mormon Trail in 1847.

Maps

By 1845 IT HAD BEEN DETERMINED THAT THE MORMONS COULD NO longer safely remain in the Illinois area. However, their leadership, under Brigham Young, had yet to determine where they would establish their new Zion. The decision had been made to move west, but not to a specific location. Earlier some had talked of Texas, Oregon, California, or the isolated area of the Great Basin. It seems that, before his death, Prophet Joseph Smith had even prophesied that their Zion would be found in the Rocky Mountains. Two major problems faced by Brigham Young and the other leaders involved the determination of the exact location where they would finally settle and the route to be used to safely bring the Mormons to their "promised land."

To a certain degree the solution was made for them. The main route west was the route used by the Oregon and California emigrants, which followed the Platte River and North Platte. Therefore, that route was the most likely choice. The emigrants and the traders before them had used a variety of jumping-off sites from the Independence, Missouri, area, north to the Council Bluffs, Iowa, area. By establishing the Mormon camp called "Winter Quarters" in the Indian lands on the west side of the Missouri and the north side of the Platte, not only were the Mormons temporarily providing themselves with some degree of safety from further persecution from the Gentiles, but it also became more likely that they would use the route along the north side of the Platte River. Research indicates that as early as June of 1846 Brigham Young was already seriously considering the Valley of the Great Salt Lake or the Bear River Valley in the Great Basin area. By mid-1847 California was ruled out in favor of the more isolated Great Basin area, and the final decision was made to settle the Valley of the Great Salt Lake. Still, in 1846, the specifics of the actual route to follow and exact location of their new Zion had yet to be determined.

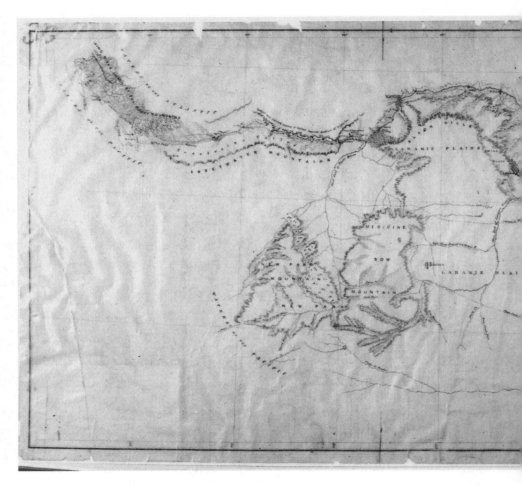

FRÉMONT-PREUSS MAP OF 1843—National Archives

36

These problems were also in part solved by the use of existing maps and guides available to the Mormons. The Mormons discussed developing their own guidebook and set of trail maps. While they did publish their own guidebook, they never developed their own set of maps. There were, however, a number of maps that played a significant role in the development of the Mormon route west during their first year of migration in 1847. The maps by John Charles Frémont and Charles Preuss, S. Augustus Mitchell, and Lansford Hastings all helped to show them the way. Even though the T. H. Jefferson map was not available until 1849, it is also included in this section because it shows nearly the whole route and was available to later emigrating Mormons.

The first significant map was the Frémont–Preuss Map of 1843. Lieutenant, and later Captain, John Charles Frémont's exploration expeditions of 1842 and then 1843–44 resulted in the trail to Oregon being recorded and mapped from Independence, Missouri, to Oregon. Charles Preuss served as his cartographer and deserves much of the credit for the high quality of their maps. Their information was incorporated into most of the maps that were produced by other cartographers. After each expedition the results were made public. The 1845 report included a map of the Valley of the Great Salt Lake. In 1846 a seven-section "Topographical Map of the Road from Missouri to Oregon" was produced and available. Its scale was ten miles to an inch. Originally it was part of Frémont's reports to Congress. More than 10,000 copies were printed and devoured by Congress and the public. Reproductions of these seven-section strip maps may still be purchased today and you can use them as you follow along the route. The 1843 map was a single large map. Joseph Smith had a copy of it in Nauvoo, and William Clayton and Brigham Young had seen it. They were also in the possession of Frémont's seven-section maps when they left from Winter Quarters in 1847 for their new promised land. While the Frémont–Preuss maps traced the route on the south side of the Platte and the Mormons largely followed the north bank of the river, the maps served as useful references once the Mormon Pioneers reached Grand Island, where Frémont's route joined the Platte River. At Fort Laramie the Mormons crossed the Platte to the south side. There they joined the established "Oregon Trail," mapped by Frémont, and generally followed it to Fort Bridger. At that point the Oregon Trail turned northwest to head for Fort Hall and then on to Oregon. The Mormons, however, headed southwest to follow the route proposed by Hastings and taken in 1846 by some California-bound companies which included emigrants George Donner, James Reed, Heinrich Lienhard, and Edwin Bryant.

Also included are portions of two of Frémont's section maps and his map of Salt Lake. The section maps show Frémont's route from Ash (Hollow) Creek on map section II where the trail meets the North Fork after the trail crosses over from the South Platte to Scotts Bluff on map section III. Scotts Bluff is located about in the middle of the map where the trail moves away from the river to bypass the bluffs that appear to come down to touch the river. That portion of the trail also coincides with the pages from Clayton's guidebook and the different diary accounts included later in the book. Look at the corresponding pictorial section also. The Frémont map of the Great Salt Lake was part of Frémont's reports to Congress and would also have been available at that time.

Another important map of 1846 was S. Augustus Mitchell's "A New Map of Texas, Oregon and California." It was available before the outcome of the Mexican War. It is considered to be the most up-to-date map produced at that time, and it included the most current information based on Frémont's, Charles Wilkes's, and William Emory's works. The only major area that was lacking in reliable detail was what was labelled "the Great Interior of California," or the Great Basin, as we know it today. There appear to have been two versions of the map produced in 1846. One minor difference is that the earlier edition had a chart listing Independence as the starting point of the Oregon route, while the later version had Westport as its beginning. Brigham Young had a copy of one of Augustus's maps for reference on his journey west. Augustus's book with its folded map was small enough to be carried in a shirt pocket. This is a close-up of the map showing the section near the Great Salt Lake. The map shows the main Oregon Trail along the North Platte, through the South Pass, over the Sublette Cutoff to the Bear River and up to and along the Snake River. It does not show the trail southwest of the South Pass to Fort Bridger which the Mormons followed.

The next item shown is the very important Lansford Hastings map copied by hand by Thomas Bullock, "Clerk of the Camp of Israel." It was copied from an original map given to Samuel Brannan and Charles Smith by Hastings in early 1847 while they were in California before their return journey to meet the main party of Mormons on their way west. They met the Mormon Pioneer Company on the Green River east of Fort Bridger and gave the map and waybill to Brigham Young. The waybill, originally written by Hastings, is included later in the guidebook section. While there had been some references to Hastings's map and waybill in Thomas Bullock's journal, they have only recently been located. While the map is rather crude compared to the maps discussed

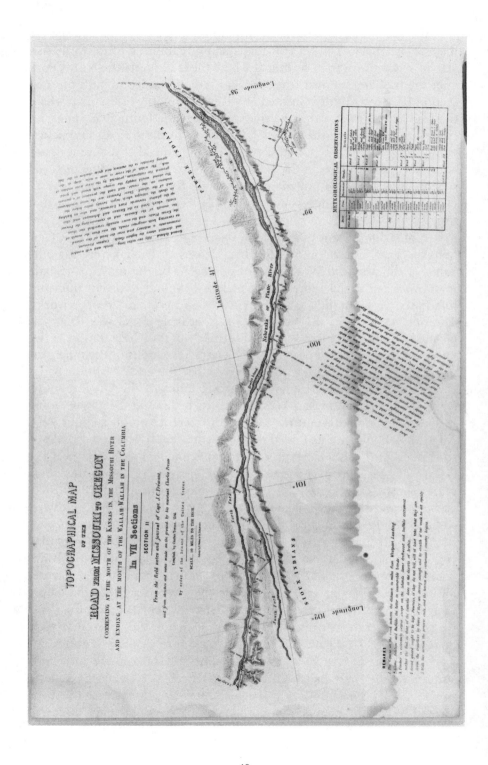

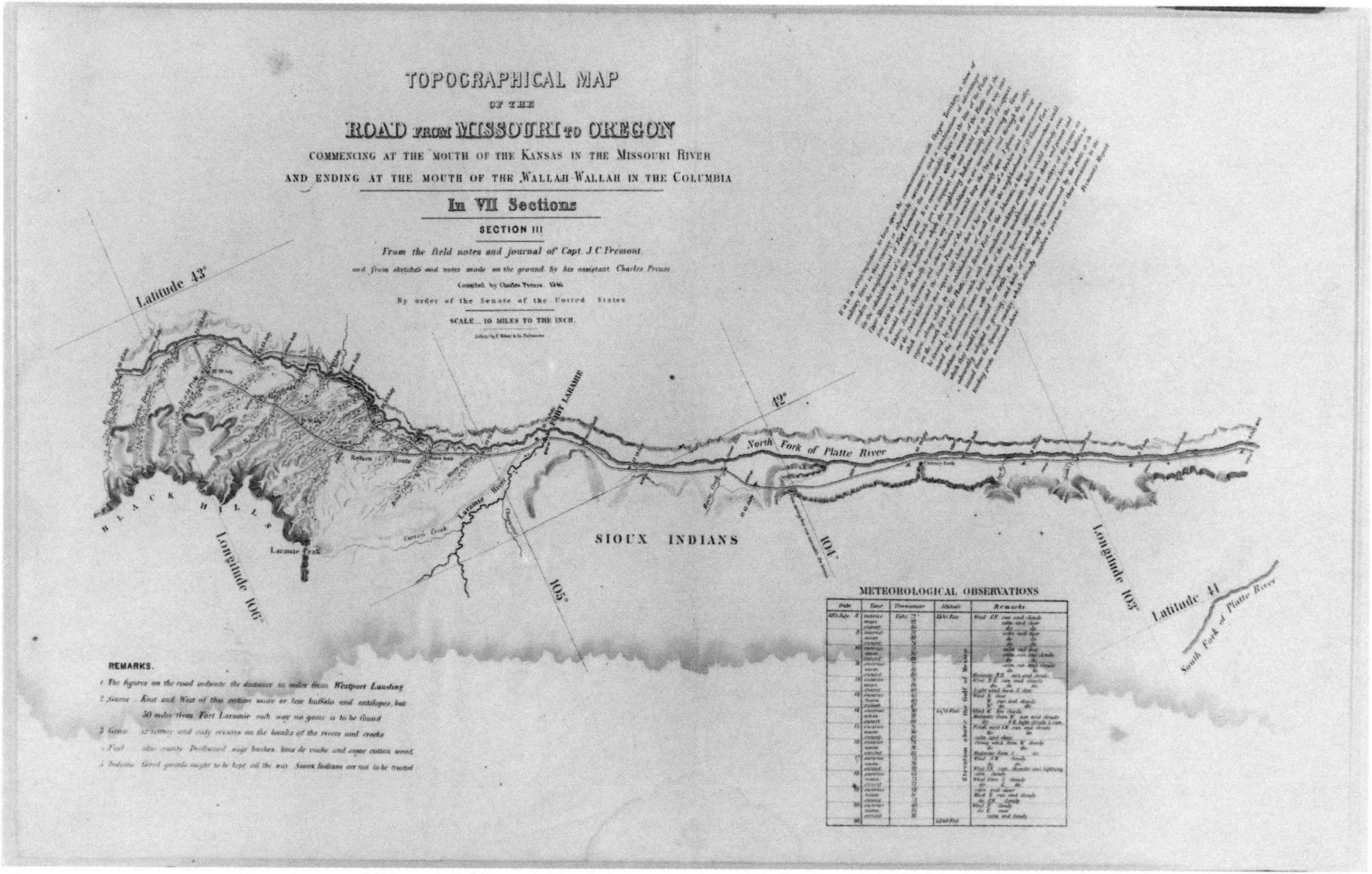

FRÉMONT STRIP MAPS—National Archives

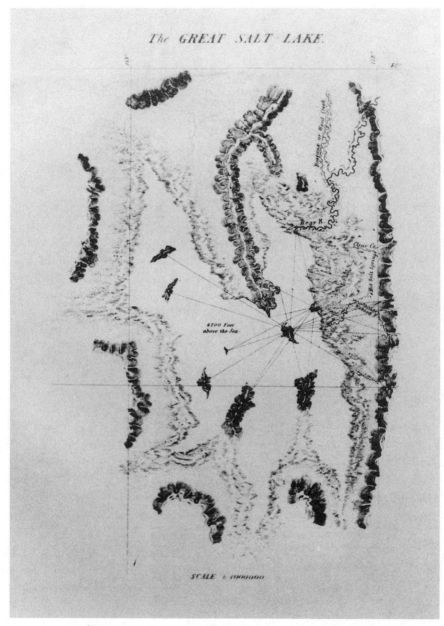

FRÉMONT MAP OF GREAT SALT LAKE—National Archives

above, it is the first copy of a map that showed the route from Fort Bridger to the Salt Lake Valley or what we now know as the end of the Mormon Trail. In recent times this last section of the Mormon Trail has also been called the Pioneer Trail.

The last map is the T. H. Jefferson map. Jefferson had gone west to California in 1846 and then returned east in 1849. He produced a four-section map of the route to California called "Map of the Emigrant Road from Independence, Mo. to St. Francisco, California." It included the route to the Great Salt Lake Valley. Only the third section of his map series is reproduced here. His first two sections are very similar to Frémont's first four sections. (All four sections of the T. H. Jefferson maps are reduced and included in my California Trail book, and the reduced copies of Frémont's seven-section maps are in my Oregon Trail book.) Jefferson had been in one of the companies that listened to Hastings's advice and took his cutoff southwest from Fort Bridger to the Valley of the Great Salt Lake and then finally farther west to meet the main California Trail. From Fort Bridger the early emigrant parties followed a route southwest to Echo Canyon down to the Weber River and Canyon. The Donner Party followed Hastings's advice to cut over the Wasatch Mountains instead of going down the very difficult Weber River Canyon. The Mormon companies followed the tracks left by the Donner wagons. Jefferson's map was not available to the first Mormon parties in 1847 and 1848, but it was available to the migrants in 1849.

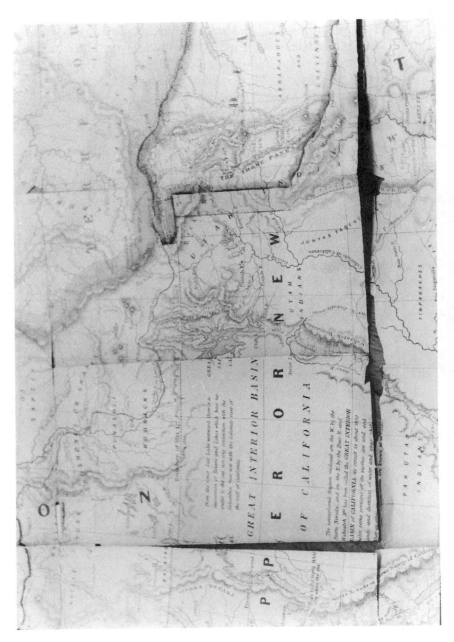

MITCHELL MAP—S. Augustus Mitchell, A

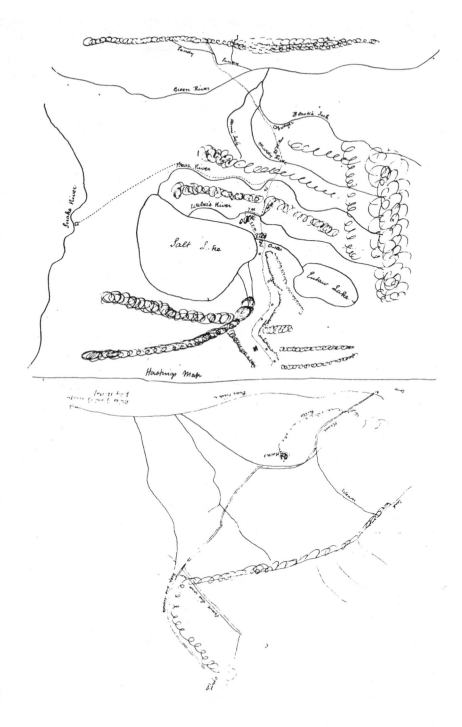

Hastings Map

45

T. H. JEFFERSON MAP—Library of Congress

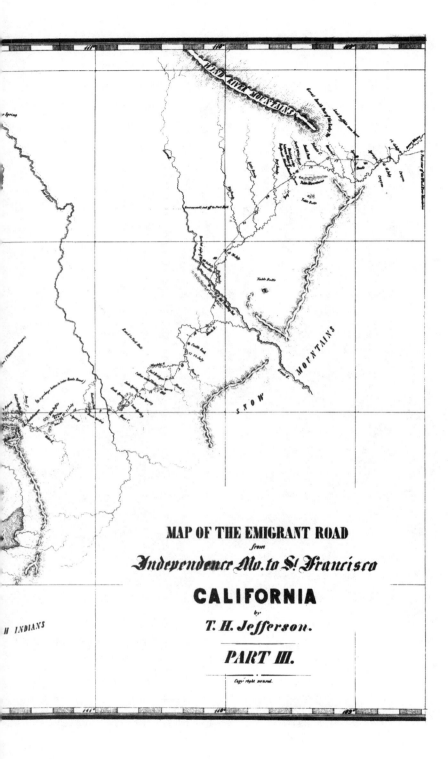

MAP OF THE EMIGRANT ROAD

from

Independence Mo. to St. Francisco

CALIFORNIA

by

T. H. Jefferson.

PART III.

Copyright secured.

WILLIAM CLAYTON—Daughters of Utah Pioneers

William Clayton joined the Mormon Church in 1831. While living in Nauvoo he became the clerk for Joseph Smith. During the exodus from Nauvoo he served as company clerk. On his march across Iowa he wrote the words to the hymn "Come, Come, Ye Saints." In 1847 he was again given the task of camp clerk for the Mormon vanguard party leaving Winter Quarters. During their trek to the Great Salt Lake Valley he helped in the development of the roadometer which accurately recorded the distance traveled. He was also given the task of writing a guidebook for future Mormon emigrants. His guidebook was one of the best available. Pages from it, as well as from his diary, are found elsewhere in this book.

Guidebooks

By 1847, when the Mormons were ready to embark on their journey west from Winter Quarters to establish their promised land, over 8,000 other emigrants had already moved west. Established trails already existed in many areas that would be followed by the emigrating Mormons. In addition to the earlier emigrants, numerous military exploratory expeditions had gone west and hundreds of trappers had been traveling back and forth along the Platte River from the mountains to the Missouri since the early 1800s. Routes had already been established to Oregon and to California with their jumping-off places located along the Missouri River in places such as the Independence-Westport area, Weston, Fort Leavenworth, St. Joseph, Nebraska City, and the Council Bluffs-Kanesville area. Thus, for most of the way, the emigrating Mormons would not be traveling through uncharted lands. However, this is not to say that guidebooks would not be useful. It seems most emigrant companies had copies of guidebooks once they became available. The better books provided the emigrants with useful information not only about the number of miles between sites, but also about the availability of grass, water, and wood. Many also provided lists of equipment and provisions that should be packed. Some even described the areas through which the emigrants would be traveling.

Among the most important sources of information about the West were Captain John Charles Frémont's reports. While Frémont's reports to Congress about his exploration expeditions to the Rocky Mountains, Oregon, and California were not published as an emigrant guide, they served the same purpose. They were the most informative and most frequently cited of the trail material available to the Mormons. In 1844 Frémont's early map and report had already been brought to the attention of Joseph Smith. After Smith's death, copies of Frémont's later maps and

reports were also read by Brigham Young and the other Mormon leaders. These reports were brought along as the Mormons moved west in
1847. They provided daily descriptions of what Frémont encountered
along the way. They appear to have been most useful to the Mormons on
the trail sections from near Grand Island to the South Pass and then in
the Great Salt Lake Valley area.

The section of Frémont's *The Exploring Expedition to the Rocky
Mountains* quoted below describes the area along the North Platte from
below Chimney Rock to Scotts Bluff as recorded July 9–11, 1842, by
Charles Preuss.

> July 9.—...Notwithstanding the confusion and excitement, we were
> very early to the road, as the days were extremely hot, and we were
> anxious to profit by the freshness of the morning. The soft marly for-
> mations, over which we were now journeying, frequently offers to the
> travellers remarkable and picturesque beauty. To several of these local-
> ities, where the winds and the rain have worked the bluffs into curious
> shapes, the voyageurs have given names according to some facial
> resemblance. One of these is called the *Court-house,* we passed about
> six miles from our encampment of last night, and towards noon came
> in sight of the celebrated *Chimney rock.* It looks, at this distance of
> thirty miles, like what it is called—the long chimney of a steam factory
> establishment, or a shot-tower in Baltimore. Nothing occurred to
> interrupt the quiet of the day, and we encamped on the river, after a
> march of twenty-four miles. Buffalo had become very scarce, and but
> one cow had been killed, of which the meat had been cut into thin
> slices, and hung around the carts to dry.
>
> July 10.—We continued along the same fine plainly beaten road,
> which the smooth surface of the country afforded us, for a distance of
> six hundred and thirty miles, from the frontiers of Missouri to the
> Laramie fork. In the course of the day we met some whites, who were
> following along the train of Mr. Bridger; and, after a day's journey of
> twenty four miles encamped about sunset at the Chimney rock, of
> which the annexed drawing will render any description unnecessary. It
> consists of marl and earthy limestone, and the weather is rapidly
> diminishing its height, which is now not more than two hundred feet
> above the river. Travellers who visited it some years since placed its
> height at upwards of five hundred feet.
>
> July 11.—The valley of the North Fork is of a variable breadth,
> from one to four, and sometimes six miles. Fifteen miles from Chim-
> ney rock we reached one of those places where the river strikes the
> bluffs, and forces the road to make a considerable circuit over the
> uplands. This presented an escarpment on the river of about nine hun-
> dred yards in length, and is familiarly known as Scott's Bluff. We have

made a journey of thirty miles before we again struck the river, at a place where some scanty grass afforded insufficient pasturage to our animals. About twenty miles from Chimney rock we had found a very beautiful spring of excellent and cold water; but it was in such a deep ravine and, so small, that the animals could not profit by it, and we therefore halted only a few minutes, and found a resting-place ten miles further on. The plain between Scott's bluffs and Chimney rock almost entirely covered with drift-wood, consisting principally of cedar, which, we were informed, had been supplied from the Black hills, in a flood of five or six years since.

Perhaps the most famous of the guidebooks available to the Mormons and other emigrants was Lansford Hastings's *The Emigrants' Guide to Oregon and California,* which was written in 1844 and published in Ohio in 1845. Hastings had originally gone to Oregon, became dissatisfied and then decided his fortune could best be made in California. It was in his guidebook that his infamous cutoff—the short cut to California by turning southwest from Fort Bridger to California—was recommended. The guide, like Frémont's reports, had been reprinted in many of the newspapers available to the Mormon and non-Mormon emigrants starting in 1845. It was also brought along and referred to on the journey to Salt Lake. Unlike Frémont's report, Hastings's guide provided only very general information about specific sections of the trail. However, a waybill handwritten by Hastings specifically for the Mormons was more useful. The waybill described the route east from Johnson's settlement in California back along the cutoff to Fort Bridger. It was sent along with the hand-drawn map of the general route from Fort Bridger across the Wasatch Mountains and Salt Lake Desert which Hastings appears to have considered the most difficult portion of his new cutoff to California. This map was the one included earlier. Here is Hastings's waybill (Korns and Morgan, *West From Fort Bridger*).

HASTINGS'S WAYBILL
ROUTE FROM MR. JOHNSON'S SETTLEMENT—
CALIFORNIA TO BRIDGER'S FORT, AS PER MR.
HASTINGS ACCOUNT

From Johnson's to Bear River Valley, 60 miles—thence to Trucker's Lake, on the other side of the mountains 40—thence down Trucky River 60—thence to the sink of Mary's River 40—thence up and along Mary's River, 250—to the forks of the Road—thence taking the right hand road, up the South Fork of Mary's River 15—Thence up a branch of the South Fork 8—thence to a sink of a small creek 7—thence up the said creek to the point where the road leaves it 5 miles—thence through a pass in the mountain 12—thence along the foot of the mountain passing numerous springs 30, to a point where the road leaves the foot of the mountain—thence 20 miles over the plain and hills to a Spring—thence 10 miles to a Spring—thence 9 miles to a Spring—thence 12 miles to a Spring—thence 25 miles to a Spring—thence 4 or 5 miles along the foot of the mountain, passing several Springs to a Spring, and a large encampment, at the west side of a Salt Plain—thence over the Salt Plain 55 miles to a Spring—thence 6 miles to a Spring—thence along and around the foot of the mountain passing numerous Springs on the West side 20 miles to a Spring on the East side—Thence keeping to the right hand road, along the foot of the mountain passing several Springs. Then bearing to the left, across the plain 20 miles, to the point of the mountain at the Salt Lake. Thence passing several Springs, and keeping [to] the right hand road, 12 miles to the Eutaw Outlet—Thence over the mountains 12 miles. Thence down a small Creek, and bearing to the right over the hills 15 miles to Weber's River—Thence up Weber River 7 miles—Thence up the Red Fork 40 miles—Thence keeping to the left hand road 25 miles to Bear River—Thence 25 miles to Bridger's Fort, on Black's Fork of Green River.

Hastings's guide, like many of the other guidebooks produced, included a list of items emigrants needed in order to outfit properly for their journey west. By 1845, a year after Joseph Smith's death, the Mormons were already preparing to leave Nauvoo because of deteriorating relations with the non-Mormons in the area. Included here is the Bill of Particulars, which was originally published in 1845 in preparation for the Mormon migration which was to leave Nauvoo in 1846. Initially, the Mormons hoped to complete their journey west in one year. However, as it turned out, the Mormon migration from Nauvoo advanced only as far as the Indian territory across the Missouri River from the Council Bluffs area. Their journey across Iowa was much more difficult than they had expected. They were forced to halt and to establish what became known as Winter Quarters on the west bank of the Missouri River and make preparations for the coming winter. This listing of items that the Mormons were recommended to pack for their journey appeared in the October 29, 1845 *Nauvoo Neighbor*.

While the Mormons did not have one guidebook for their 1847 journey, a decision was made to carefully record their progress and prepare a detailed guidebook for the Mormons who were to follow later. The task of keeping accurate records and preparing a guidebook was given to William Clayton. He served as "Clerk of the Camp of Israel" when the first Mormons left Nauvoo and traveled to their Winter Quarters. When the

BILL OF PARTICULARS

Each family consisting of five persons, to be provided with

1 good strong wagon, well covered with a light box.

2 or 3 good yoke of oxen between the age of 4 and 10 years.

2 or more milch cows.

1 or more good beeves.

3 sheep if they can be obtained.

1000 lbs. of flour or other bread or bread stuffs in good sacks.

1 good musket or rifle to each male over the age of 12 years.

1 lb. Powder,

4 do Lead,

1 do Tea,

5 do Coffee.

100 do Sugar,

4 do Cayenne Pepper,

2 do Black do,

4 do Mustard,

10 do Rice for each family,

1 do Cinnamon,

4 do Cloves,

1 doz Nutmegs,

25 lbs Salt,

5 do Saleratus,

10 do Dried apples.

4 bush. of Beans.

A few lbs of dried Beef or Bacon.

5 lbs dried Peaches,

20 do do Pumpkin,

25 do Seed grain,

1 gal. Alcohol,

20 lbs of Soap each family,

4 or 5 Fish hooks and lines for do.

15 lbs. Iron and Steel.

A few lbs of wrought nails,

One or more sets of saw or grist mill Irons to company of 100 families,

2 sets of Pully Blocks and ropes to each co'y for crossing rivers,

1 good Seine and hook for each company,

From 25 to 100 lbs of Farming & mechanical tools,

Cooking utentials to consist of a Bake kettle, frying pan, coffee pot, & tea kettle;

Tin cups, plates, knives forks, spoons, & pans as few as will do.

A good tent and furniture to each 2 families.

Clothing & bedding to each family not to exceed 500 pounds.

Ten extra teams for each company of 100 families.

N. B. In addition to the above list, horse and mule teams, can be used as well as oxen. Many items of comfort and convenience will suggust themselves to a wise and provident people, and can be laid in in season; but none should start without filling the original bill.

**BILL OF PARTICULARS—LDS Archives
(Note: On the listing, "do" means "ditto.")**

PROMINENT POINTS AND REMARKS.	Dist. miles.	From W Qrs. miles.	From C of G S L miles.
Duck-weed creek, 10 feet wide. - - Abundance of good, cold spring water, Oct. 1, 1847.	¾	346¾	684¼
Shoal stream, 3 feet wide. - - - Dry, October 1, 1847.	2	348¾	682¼
Rattlesnake creek, 20 feet wide, 1½ ft. deep. Swift current, sandy bottom, but not bad to cross.	3¾	352¼	678¼
Cedar Bluffs. - - - - - On the south side the river. Lat. 41° 13′ 44″ Long 101° 52′	1½	354	677
Creek, six feet wide. - - - - Water plenty, September 30, 1847. Land, in this neighborhood, sandy.	5	359	672
Creek, four feet wide. - - - Plenty of water, September 30, 1847.	¼	359¼	671¾
Crooked Creek, five feet wide. - - Plenty of water, September 30, 1847.	½	359¾	671¼
Camp Creek, eight feet wide. - - Two creeks here, about the same size, but a few rods apart—water cold and plenty, September 30, 1847. No doubt they rise from springs.	4	363¾	667¼
Creek, three feet wide. - - - Plenty of water, May 20, but dry, September 30, 1847	4	367¾	663¼
Pond Creek, four feet wide. - - Dry, September 30, near the river, but further north many ponds and tall grass.	¼	368	663
Wolf Creek, 20 feet wide. - - - At the east foot of Sandy Bluffs, which are bad to cross, you will probably have to double teams, if heavy loaded.	1½	369¼	661¼
Sandy Bluffs, west foot. Two hundred yard further, is a creek five feet wide.	¾	370¼	660¾
Watch Creek, 8 feet wide, and 2 feet deep. After this, the road runs pretty near the river banks, to avoid some swamps near the bluffs.	3½	373¾	657¼
"Lone Tree," north side the river. - About three hundred yards south from the road.	4½	378	653
Ash Hollow, south side the river. - So named from a grove of Ash timber growing on it. It occupies a space of about fifteen or twenty acres, and is surrounded by high bluffs.	2½	380¼	650¾
Castle Creek, 6 rods wide, 2 feet deep. Swift current, quick sand bottom, water muddy. Low banks, but not good to cross, on account of quick sands.	3	383¾	647¼
Castle Bluffs, south side the river. - You cross no more creeks of water until you arrive at Crab creek, twenty-five and a half miles from here. The road good, except in one place, where you travel three fourths of a mile over sand	4½	388	643
Sand Hill creek, 12 feet wide, south side the road. - - - - - Near some sandy mounds, on the north side the road.	¾	388¾	642¼
Creek or slough. - - - - Dry.	1½	390¼	640¾
Creek or slough. - - - - Dry.	7½	397¾	633¼
Sandy Bluffs, east foot. - - -	3	400¾	630¼

CLAYTON'S GUIDE

PROMINENT POINTS AND REMARKS.	DIST. miles.	From W Qrs. miles.	From C of G S L. miles.
Sandy Bluffs, west foot. - - -	¾	401¼	629¾
Dry creek. - - - - -	¼	401½	629½
Dry do. - - - - -	¾	402¼	628¾
Dry creek, 30 feet wide. - - -	4	406¼	624¾
The road runs near the river, from here to Crab creek.			
Crab Creek, 20 feet wide, very shoal. -	3	409¼	621¾
Two miles further you will see some high bluffs on the right. By ascending one of the highest you will see Chimney Rock, to the west.			
Small lake, south of the road. - -	1¼	410½	620½
Good chance to camp, without turning from the road.			
Cobble Hills, east foot. - - -	5	415½	615½
You cross three dry creeks before you arrive here and then you travel over another range of sandy bluffs—ascent pretty steep, but not very sandy.			
Cobble Hills, west foot. - - -	2¼	417¾	613¼
After you descend on the low land, you will find it mostly sandy for ten miles, and in some places very heavy drawing.			
"Ancient Bluff Ruins," north side the road. Latitude 41° 33′ 3″. - - -	1¼	419	612
Resembling the ruins of ancient castles, fortifications, &c.; but visitors must be cautious, on account of the many rattle-snakes lurking round, and concealed in the clefts of the bluffs.			
R. and R., road joins the river. - -	10½	429½	601½
Good place to camp. After this, the road runs near the river, until you arrive at the next low sandy ridges.			
Low sandy bluffs, east foot. - -	7½	437	594
Low sandy bluffs, west foot. - -	1	438	593
After this, the land for several miles, is soft in wet weather, but good traveling in dry weather.			
"Chimney Rock," (meridian) south side the river. - - - - - -	14½	452½	578½
The higher land now begins to be sandy and barren. Many Prickly-pears and Wild Sage, which continue mostly through the remainder of the journey.			
Scott's Bluffs, (mer.) south side the river.	19½	472	559
The road here is near enough to the river to camp. Lat. of meridian 41° 50′ 52″; Long. 103° 20′.			
Spring Creek, 10 feet wide, 8 inches deep.	4	476	555
South of the road. You do not cross it, but travel half a mile alongside. Good water, and many trout in it.			
R. and R., road runs near the river. -	12½	488½	542½
Good chance to camp.			
Low sandy bluffs, north side the road. -	2¾	491¼	539¾
You travel at the foot of these bluffs, but will find the road sandy and heavy on teams.			
Creek, about 200 yards south of road. -	2	493¼	537¾
By ascending one of the highest bluffs near, you have a view of "Laramie Peak" in the Black Hills.			
Timber, north side the river. - -	11½	504¾	526¼
Road here about a quarter of a mile from the river—after this generally from one to two miles distant. The road to Laramie very sandy.			
"Raw Hide" creek, 1 rod wide. : -	5¼	510	521
Plenty of water, June 1st, but dry, Sept 15 1847.			

vanguard company of Mormons left their Winter Quarters on April 15, 1847, he was appointed to assist Thomas Bullock, the official clerk, in keeping a detailed record of their journey and daily progress. Within a few days it became evident that they needed a precise method for measuring the distance traveled. First, he tried estimation; then he tried counting wheel revolutions; and finally he used a "roadometer," a mechanical device that counted wheel revolutions to measure distance. It was jointly developed by Clayton, Orson Pratt, and Appleton Harmon. The device was installed on May 12 and from then on his records were extremely accurate. After he arrived in Salt Lake Valley, he was assigned to prepare a table of distances between Salt Lake and Winter Quarters and a map to complement it. He started on his return trip and again measured and recorded information which he used in his guidebook. Five thousand copies of his guide, *The Latter-Day Saints Emigrants' Guide*, were initially printed. It was an instant success. Not only was it in demand by Mormons, but non-Mormons also used it, and even other authors of guidebooks "freely" copied sections of his book and incorporated them into their own guidebooks. Two pages of Clayton's guide are included here. Note the milepost approach and detail. There is no evidence, however, that he prepared a corresponding map.

These two pages from Clayton's guide correspond to the section of the journey described in the diary section and also shown on the Frémont Section Maps. Ash Hollow is at mile 380 3/4 from Winter Quarters and Scotts Bluff is at mile 472.

In later years Mormon wagon companies did not always follow the same route. As a result they often relied on other guidebooks besides Clayton's. Hosea Horn's guide was used by Frederick Piercy in 1853. Horn's guide started at Council Bluffs, followed the north side of the river until reaching Fort Laramie, where it crossed over to the south side. Piercy, however, followed the north side of the Platte River all the way to central Wyoming, never crossing to the south side near Fort Laramie. This route has often been called Chiles's Route. On his way back, however, Piercy did travel on the south side.

Diaries

WHILE MANY EMIGRANTS RECORDED THE EVENTS OF THEIR JOURNEYS IN their diaries, most did not. It is estimated that perhaps only one in 200 to 250 emigrants recorded the events of the trip. Our knowledge about what it was like traveling in a wagon company is based on those diarists, and most of them have not been published, nor are they available for the general population. Also, most of those diaries are rather short summaries from a few sentences to a paragraph, noting the mileage and perhaps a couple of events of daily travel. Only a few are truly detailed accounts of daily occurrences. One of the most detailed accounts was J. Goldsborough Bruff's 1849 diary of his wagon company's trip to California. In recent years, more diaries have been published for the general public.

In most respects Mormon emigrants were similar to non-Mormon emigrants. Most did not record their journey, and most of those who did write seem to have written brief accounts. There appears to be no reason to explain the existence of detailed non-Mormon, or Gentile, diaries except for the individual desires of some emigrants. However, the Mormon companies, because of their more formal organization often specifically assigned one or more persons the responsibility for recording the progress and daily events of their journey. They may have been assigned to act either as the official clerk of the camp or as the clerk or diarist for one of the leaders of the company.

In this section there are excerpts from three diarists: William Clayton, 1847; Patty Sessions, 1847; and Frederick H. Piercy, 1853. All three are representative of emigrant diaries. Each describes the journey along the portion of the trail on the north side of the North Platte River across from the landmarks between Ash Hollow and Scotts Bluff. Step back in time as they tell you what their journey was like.

William Clayton served as the clerk of the camp that left Nauvoo in 1846. In 1847 he was assigned to assist Thomas Bullock, camp clerk, in recording the events of the Mormon Pioneer Company that led the departure from the Winter Quarters and first entered and settled in the Great Salt Lake Valley. He was also asked to serve as scribe for church leader Heber Kimball by keeping Kimball's diary along with his own. His personal diary, quoted here (Clayton, *William Clayton's Journal*), is the most comprehensive of the three and one of the best of the whole Mormon Trail period. He left Winter Quarters on April 14 and arrived in the Great Salt Lake Valley on July 22.

Diary Entries: Thursday, [May] 20th– Thursday, [May] 27th [1847]

THURSDAY, 20TH. The morning fair, but cloudy, light wind from northwest and cold. At 7:45 we started out again but had not traveled over a quarter of a mile before the roadometer gave way on account of the rain yesterday having caused the wood to swell and stick fast. One of the cogs in the small wheel broke. We stopped about a half an hour and Appleton Harmon took it to pieces and put it up again without the small wheel. I had to count each mile after this. Three quarters of a mile from where we camped, we crossed a creek eight feet wide and two and a half feet deep. We then changed our course to about southwest a mile or so following the banks of the river, as the ground was wet and swampy nearer the bluffs. The river then winds around about three miles in a bend and then strikes a little north of west. The bluffs on the north appear to be about two miles from the river. We traveled till 11:15 and then halted to feed, having traveled seven and three quarters miles over tolerably good road, though at the commencement somewhat soft. On the opposite side the river, the bluffs project near its banks. They are rocky and almost perpendicular, beautified for miles by groves of cedar. Opposite to where we are halted, we can see a ravine running up the bluffs and at the foot, a flat bottom of about fifteen acres. At the farther side of this bottom is a grove of trees not yet in leaf. Brother Brown thinks they are ash and that the place is what is called Ash Hollow and on Fremont's map, Ash Creek. We all felt anxious to ascertain the fact whether this is Ash Hollow or not, for if it is, the Oregon Trail strikes the river at this place, and if it can be ascertained that such is the fact, we then have a better privilege of testing Fremont's distances to Laramie. We have already discovered that his map is not altogether correct in several respects, and particularly in showing the windings of the river and the distance of the bluffs from it. I suggested the propriety of some persons going over in the boat and Brother John Brown suggested it to President Young. The boat was soon hauled by the brethren to the river and Orson Pratt, Amasa Lyman, Luke Johnson and John Brown started to row over, but the current was so exceedingly strong the oars had no effect. John Brown then jumped into the river which was about two and a half feet deep and dragged the boat over, the others assisting with the oars. After some hard labor they arrived on the opposite shore and went to the hollow. They soon found the Oregon Trail and ascertained that this is Ash Hollow, Brother Brown having traveled on that road to near Laramie last season with the Mississippi company and knew the place perfectly well. They gathered some branches of wild cherry in full bloom, rambled over the place a little while and then returned to camp. About the same time the camp prepared to pursue their journey. The brethren arrived and made their report, and at 1:45 p.m. we proceeded onward. From the appearance of the bluffs ahead, our course this afternoon will be west and northwest. A light breeze from northwest. Soon after we started, one of the brethren killed a large rattlesnake within a rod of the road made by the wagons and on the side where the cows travel. He killed it to prevent its injuring the cows and threw it away from the road. In the river one and a quarter miles above Ash Hollow, there are several small islands on which grow many trees of cedar. One of these islands is perfectly green over with cedar and looks beautiful. The bluffs also on the south side the river continue to be lined with cedar apparently for two miles yet and are very high and almost perpendicular, running pretty close to the river. On this side the river, the bluffs seem to bear farther to the north, being apparently about three miles from the river, and a few miles farther west they are as much as five miles from the river. After traveling three and a quarter miles from the noon stop, we crossed a tributary stream running into the Platte, in a very crooked direction, being from four to eight rods wide and two and a half feet deep most of the way across, the bottom quick sand, current rapid and water of sandy color, like the Platte. Some had to double teams to get over, but all got over safely. We proceeded on about four miles farther and found that the river bends considerably to the north. The bluffs also bend to the south, so that the low bluffs in front almost reach the banks only barely leaving room for a road. We went a little farther and camped for the night at half past five, having traveled this afternoon eight miles, making fifteen and three quarters miles during the day. Elder Kimball and several others went forward on horses to pick out our road as usual. I have seen several kinds of herbs growing today which appear new to me. One looks like a penny royal, smells almost like it, but tastes hot and like the oil of cloves. Elder Kimball and others saw a very large wolf about half a mile west, and he appeared to be following them to camp. They turned and rode up to him and round him, struck their pistols at him, but they did not go off, being damp. He finally made his escape. The large stream we crossed this afternoon is named Castle Creek from the bluffs on the opposite side which much resemble the rock on which Lancaster Castle is built. The bluffs are named Castle Bluffs. We had a light shower this afternoon, but the evening is fine though very cool.

FRIDAY, 21ST. The morning very fine and pleasant though tolerably cold. I put up a guide board at this place with the following inscriptions on it: 'From Winter Quarters 409 miles. From the junction of the North and South Forks, 93 1/4 miles. From Cedar Bluffs, south side the river, 36 1/2 miles. Ash Hollow, south side the river, 8 miles. Camp of the Pioneers May 21, 1847. According to Fremont, this place is 132 miles from Laramie. N.B. The bluffs opposite are named Castle Bluffs.' At 7:35 we continued our journey. We found the prairie tolerably wet, many ponds of water standing which must have been caused by a heavy fall of rain, much more heavy than we had back. However, it was not very bad traveling. We made a pretty straight road this morning at about the distance of a mile from the river. The bluffs on the north appear to be five miles or over from our road. At 11:15 we halted for dinner, having traveled nearly seven and three quarters miles, course north of northwest, very warm and no wind. Presidents Young and Kimball rode forward to pick the road, and near this place they saw a nest of wolves, caught and killed two with sticks. Four or five others escaped to their hole. At half past one we proceeded onward and found the prairie wet, and grass high of last year's growth. After traveling four and three quarters miles we arrived at a range of low bluffs projecting to the river, which at this place bends to the north. There is, however, a bottom of about a rod wide between the bluffs and the river, but as it is wet and soft, it was preferred to cross over the bluffs by bending a little more to the north. We traveled on the bluffs a little over a quarter of a mile and then turned on the bottom again. The bluffs are low and almost as level as the bottom. After we crossed the bluffs we found the road better. We saw about a mile this side of the foot of the bluffs, a very large bone almost petrified into stone. Most of the brethren believe it to be the shoulder bone of a mammoth, and is very large indeed. About this time a badger was brought to the wagons which Brother Woodruff had killed. As I was walking along and looking over the river, I heard a rattlesnake, and looking down saw that I had stepped within a foot of it. It rattled hard but seemed to make way. We threw it away from the track without killing it. At five o'clock Elder Kimball rode up and stopped the forward teams till the last ones got nearer saying that some Indians had come down from the bluffs to the brethren ahead. When the rest of the wagons came up we moved on a quarter of a mile farther and at half past five formed our encampment in a circle with the wagons close together as possible, having traveled seven and three quarters miles this afternoon, making fifteen and a half through the day. As the camp was forming two Indians came nearer, being a man and his squaw. They represented by signs that they were Sioux and that a party of them are now on the bluffs north of us and not far distant. By the aid of glasses we could see several on the bluffs with their ponies, evidently watching our movements. This man was hunting when first seen and appeared afraid when he saw the brethren. The squaw fled for the bluffs as fast as her horse could go, but by the signs made to them they gathered courage and came up. President Young gave orders not to bring them into camp, and they soon rode off to the bluffs. The man has got a good cloth coat on and appears well dressed. The horses they rode are said to be work horses which makes us suspect they have stolen them from travelers. The day has been very warm and some of the teams gave out. We can see some timber on the bluffs on the other side of the river some miles ahead which is the first timber we have seen for more than a week, except some small cedar and timber in Ash Hollow, all on the south side of the river. We are nearly a mile from water and the brethren have to dig wells to obtain a supply for cooking. The feed here is very poor, not much but old grass. Our course this afternoon has been a little north of west. Lorenzo Young shot two very large ducks with one ball and brought them to camp. Elder Kimball proposed tonight that I should leave a number of pages for so much of his journal as I am behind in copying and start from the present and keep it up daily. He furnished me a candle and I wrote the journal of this day's travel by candle light in his journal, leaving fifty-six pages blank. The evening was very fine and pleasant. The latitude at noon halt 41° 24' 5".

SATURDAY, 22ND. Morning beautiful, no wind and warm. We have not been disturbed by the Indians; all is peace in the camp. At eight o'clock we continued our journey, making a more crooked road than usual, having to bend south to near the banks of the river. The prairie somewhat soft and a little uneven. After traveling five and a half miles we crossed a very shoal creek about twenty feet wide. The bluffs and river about a mile apart, but on the other side, the bluffs recede two miles back from the river and have lost their craggy and steep appearance, the ascent being gradual, while on this side they begin to be rocky, cragged and almost perpendicular though not very high. We traveled till half past eleven and then halted for noon, having traveled seven and a quarter miles, the road on this side the creek being better. Our course about west of northwest with a light breeze from the east. Elder Kimball and others ahead as usual. The creek above mentioned was named Crab Creek because some of the brethren saw a very large crab in it. A mile east of this creek is a dry creek, down which, from appearances, a heavy stream runs at some seasons of the year, perhaps during heavy storms. The water running from the bluffs swells it to a considerable height and it is certain there are tremendous storms here. A while after we halted, Porter Rockwell came in and said he had been on the high bluff about a mile northwest of us and had seen the rock called Chimney Rock which appeared a long distance off. We have been in hopes to come in sight of it today and feel anxious in order to ascertain more certainly the correctness of Fremont's distance. In order to satisfy myself, although my feet were blistered and very sore, I determined to take my telescope and go on the bluff to ascertain for myself whether the noted rock could be seen or not. At half past twelve I started out alone. I found the distance to the foot of the bluff a good mile, the ascent gradual. From the foot the bluff looks very high and rough, many huge rocks having broken from the summit from time to time and rolled down a long distance. I found the ascent very steep and lengthy in comparison to its appearance from camp. When I arrived on the top I found a nice slightly arched surface of about a quarter of an acre in extent, but barren and very little grass on it. Huge comparatively smooth rocks peeped through the surface on one of which I wrote with red chalk: 'Wm. Clayton, May 22, 1847.' On the highest point I sat down and took a view of the surrounding country which is magnificent indeed. On the south side at a distance of two miles from the river, there is a range of cedar trees on the bluffs which very much resemble some of the parks and seats of gentry in England. East I could see where we camped last night, the high grass still burning. Northeast, north, and northwest, alternately, appeared high swelling bluffs and valleys as far as the eye could see or the glass magnify. West, the course of the Platte for ten or fifteen miles and at about four or five miles distance, a large bend to the north brings it in contact with the bluffs on this side. At the distance, I should judge of about twenty miles, I could see Chimney Rock very plainly with the naked eye, which from here very much resembles the large factory chimneys in England, although I could not see the form of its base. The rock lay about due west from here. After gratifying my curiosity, and seeing the men collecting their teams for a march, I descended on the west side of the bluff. The descent at this point looks more alarming than on the other. The side being very steep and all along huge rocks standing so critically, that to all appearance, a waft of wind would precipitate them to the prairie below with tremendous force. In one place in particular, a ponderous mass of rock appears to hang from the edge of the bluff without any visible means of being retained in its position, and by grazing at it a little while, it is easy to imagine you can see it move and ready to overwhelm you instantly. At a little distance from the base of the bluff, I turned to gaze on the romantic scenery above and was struck at the appearance of a large rock projecting from one corner, which very much resembled a frog's head of immense size with its mouth part open. The thought was, those bluffs ought to be named and what name more appropriate than Frog's Head Bluffs. After this reflection, I walked on to where I thought the wagons would come which started out at half past one. After traveling three and a quarter miles we crossed a dry creek about six rods wide, and a quarter of a mile farther, another about five feet wide and a half a mile farther, still another about six rods wide on an average. These all appear to be the sources of heavy streams of water at some seasons of the year. Soon as we crossed this last one, I saw Elder Kimball wave his hat for the wagons to turn off to the north in order to cross the bluffs which struck the river a little farther. But a little to the west was a very high ridge and I concluded to walk on to it. Found it to be a perfect ridge of gravel, very high and rounding on the top, not more than four or five feet wide and from north to south about 150 feet long. Elder Pratt names this Cobble Hills, the gravel or cobbles varying in size of from fifty pounds in weight to the smallest pebble. At the north foot of this hill is what might be named a clay bank, being composed of a light colored kind of sandy clay and forms a kind of large table. A little distance farther, we crossed another dry creek about eight rods wide and then ascended the bluffs. The ascent is pretty steep for nearly half a mile, but hard and not difficult to travel. The wagon had to wind about some to keep around the foot of the bluffs, crossing the dry creek three times before we emerged from the bluffs to the banks of the river. We crossed another dry creek pretty steep on each side and then found ourselves once more on the prairie bottom. The bluffs are two and a quarter miles from the east to the west foot following our trail. The wind has blown from the southeast all day until lately, when a dead calm has succeeded. In the west a heavy thunder cloud has been gathering for two hours and vivid streaks of lightning observed in the distance. At twenty minutes to five the wind struck suddenly from the northwest, the blackest part of the cloud then lying in that direction. We had a few drops of rain only. Then it seemed to turn off to the east. The scenery after this was indeed sublime, the sun peering out from under the heavy clouds reflecting long rays upwards which were imitated in the east. The romantic bluffs on the north and the lightning playing in the southeast all tended to fill my mind with pleasant reflections, on the goodness and majesty of the Creator and Governor of the universe, and the beauty of the works of his hands. At 5:45 we formed our encampment in a circle within a quarter of a mile of the banks of the river, having traveled this afternoon, eight and a quarter miles and through the day fifteen and a half, making the distance from Winter Quarters 440 miles in five weeks and three and a half days. The feed on the lower bench of the prairie is tolerably good, while the higher land is quite bare. We have noticed today a great many petrified bones, some very large. All are turned into a solid, hard, stone, which proves that the atmosphere is pure and the country would doubtless be healthy, but is not adapted for farming purposes on account of the poor sandy soil and no timber at all on this side of the river. I have noticed a variety of shrubs, plants and flowers all new to me today, many of which have a pleasant smell and in some places the air appears impregnated with the rich odors arising from them. Among the rest are numerous beds of the southern wood. There are also vast beds of flinty pebbles of various colors, some as white as alabaster. About 6:30 I observed a group of brethren standing together inside the camp. I went up and saw a young eagle which had been taken out of its nest on one of these high bluffs by George R. Grant and Orson Whitney. Although it is very young and its feathers have scarcely commenced growing, it measures from the tips of its wings when stretched, forty-six inches. Its head is nearly the size of my fist and looks ferocious. After this I went with John Pack and Horace Whitney to the bluffs. On our way we saw a large wolf about as large as the largest dog in camp. He was within a quarter of a mile from camp. After traveling about a mile we arrived at the foot of a stupendous mass of rocks almost perpendicular, with only one place where it was possible to ascend. We went up with difficulty and by using our hands and knees, gained the top. We had to walk over a little space which was only about three feet wide and on the east side a perpendicular fall of about sixty feet. Although from the camp this peak looks only large enough for a man to stand upon we found it large enough to seat comfortably about twenty persons. The top is composed of large rocks and very uneven. The prairie below looks a long distance under foot from this peak. Descending we viewed the surrounding scenery which looks more like the ruins of an ancient city with its castles, towers, fortifications, etc., on all sides, and a dry stream coming through the center. We proceeded to the next high rock and found it very difficult of ascent. The top is nearly level and very pleasant. We discovered several other varieties of shrubbery, all smelling pleasant and strong. We saw that a horse has sometimes stood on the top, but how he got there, we could not easily determine. At the east end there is a cedar tree flat on the top and on the underside almost like an umbrella. We made a calculation of the height of this bluff as well as we could and concluded it must be at least 200 feet higher than the river. The surrounding country can be seen for many miles from its summit, and Chimney Rock shows very plainly. We descended at the east end and arrived in camp at dark well satisfied with our journey. Some of the brethren have discovered a cave in one of these bluffs, and one went into it a little distance, but it being very dark and having no torch, he did not venture far. Elder Pratt reports that he saw on the top of one of the bluffs, a hole in a rock 15 inches in diameter and a foot deep with five inches of very cold good water in it. He supposed it to be a spring. Between the bluffs they also discovered a spring of pure cold water of a very good taste. Dr. Richards names these bluffs "Bluff Ruins" from their appearance being that of the ruins of castles, cities, etc. A little to the left is a small perpendicular rock much resembling Chimney Rock but smaller.

The whole of the scenery around is one of romantic beauty which cannot be described with either pen or tongue. Last night a large black dog, half wolf, supposed to belong to the Indians, came to camp. He has kept within two hundred yards of the wagons all day, and has followed us to this place. There have been many rattlesnakes seen today and six or seven killed. In fact, this place seems to abound with them. The evening was spent very joyfully by most of the brethren, it being very pleasant and moonlight. A number danced till the bugle sounded for bed time at nine o'clock. A mock trial was also prosecuted in the case of the camp vs. James Davenport for blockading the highway and turning ladies out of their course. Jackson Redding acted as the presiding judge. Elder Whipple attorney for defendant and Luke Johnson attorney for the people. We have many such trials in the camp which are amusing enough and tend among other things to pass away the time cheerfully during leisure moments. It was remarked this evening that we have one man in camp who is entitled to the credit of being more even tempered than any of the others, and that is Father Chamberlain. He is invariably cross and quarrelsome, but the brethren all take it as a joke and he makes considerable amusement for the camp. Opposite the encampment there are quite a number of small islands, but no timber on any of them.

SUNDAY, 23RD. The morning very fine and pleasant. Brother Egan commenced washing very early on the banks of the river. He kindly volunteered to wash my dirty clothing which I accepted as a favor. After breakfast President Young, Elders Kimball, Richards, Pratt, Woodruff, Smith and Benson and Lyman walked out to view Bluff Ruins and returned at half past eleven. A while ago I went out a little distance to view an adder which George Billings had discovered. It was a dark brown color about 18 inches long and three quarters of an inch thick through the body. They are represented as very poisonous. About eleven o'clock Nathaniel Fairbanks came into camp having been bitten in the leg by a rattlesnake. He went on the bluffs with Aaron Farr and Brother Rolf and as they jumped off from the bluff, the snake bit him, the others having jumped over him farther. He said that in two minutes after he was bitten his tongue began to prick and feel numb. When he got to camp his tongue and hands pricked and felt numb as a person feels their feet sometimes when they are said to be asleep. The brethren immediately applied some tobacco juice and leaves, also turpentine, and bound tobacco on his leg which was considerably swollen. We laid hands on him and Luke Johnson administered a dose of lobelia in number six after he had taken a strong drink of alcohol and water. The lobelia soon vomitted him powerfully. He complains much of sickness at his stomach and dimness in his eyes. He appears to be in much pain. While the brethren of the quorum of the twelve were on one of the high detached bluffs they found the skeleton of a buffalo's head.

Brother Woodruff wrote the names of all the quorum of the twelve present and set it upon the southwest corner of the bluff. John Brown also wrote his name on it. Elder Pratt took the altitude of the bluff and found it to be 235 feet above the surface of the river. He did not calculate the height above the sea, owing to the state of the atmosphere. He, however, predicted wind from the same cause. At twelve o'clock the camp was called together for meeting, and after singing and praying we were addressed by Elder Snow, followed by President Young. The latter said there were many items of doctrine which he often felt like teaching to the brethren, but as to administering sealing ordinances, etc., this is no time or place for them, they belong to the house of God and when we get located we shall have an opportunity to build a house, etc. He expressed himself satisfied with the conduct of the camp in general. He is pleased to see so much union and disposition to obey council among the brethren and hoped and prayed that it may continue and increase. He wants the brethren to seek after knowledge and be faithful to acknowledge God in all things but never take his name in vain nor use profane language. If all the knowledge in this camp were put together and brother Joseph were here in our midst, he could comprehend the whole of it and wind it around his little finger. And then think of the knowledge of angels, and above that, the knowledge of the Lord. There is much for us to learn and a faithful man who desires eternal glory will seek after knowledge all the time and his ideas never suffered to rust but are always bright. He will not throw away the knowledge of small things because they are familiar, but grasp all he can and keep doing so and by retaining many small things he will thus gain a large pile, etc. He expressed his feelings warmly towards all the brethren and prayed them to be faithful, diligent and upright, for we are now sowing seed, the fruit of which will be plucked in after days whether good or bad. G.A. Smith made a few remarks, also several others of the brethren. The president then stated that on Sunday next he wants the brethren to understand that there will be meeting at eleven o'clock and the sacrament administered, and he wants the brethren to attend, all that can, and not ramble off and fatigue themselves but use the Sabbath as a day of rest. He enjoined it upon Bishops T. Lewis, S. Roundy, J.S. Higbee and A. Everett to see that the proper necessities were prepared for the sacrament. The meeting was then dismissed. A while after meeting I walked out with Elder Kimball a piece from the camp. We sat down and I read to him, my journal of the last four days with which he seemed well pleased. We then knelt down together and poured out our souls to God for ourselves, the camp and our dear families in Winter Quarters. While we were engaging in prayer the wind rose suddenly from the northwest, a heavy cloud having been gathering from the west all the afternoon. A sudden gust struck Elder Kimball's hat and carried it off. After we got through, his hat was nowhere in sight, but following the direction of the wind we soon saw it at a distance on the bottom of the prairie still flying swiftly. We both ran and chased it about three quarters of a mile and caught it a little from the river. While we were out together I remarked that the buffalo gnat had bitten us very severely. Elder Kimball said they bit him very badly last evening. Their bite is very poisonous, and although they are extremely small, they punish a person very much with an itching, aching pain like a mosqui-toe bite. About five o'clock the wind blew a perfect gale and continued till seven when it commenced to rain very heavily, large drops descend-ing, accompanied with hail, which however, did not continue very long but the wind continued nearly all night. The lightning and thunder continued some time but not very severe. We saw the necessity of hav-ing good stout bows to our wagons, and the covers well fastened down, for the very stoutest seemed in danger of being torn to pieces and the wagons blown over. When the wind commenced blowing so strongly it turned very cold and long before dark I went to bed to keep warm. Brother Fairbanks seems considerably better. This evening President Young, Kimball and Benson laid hands on him and he seemed much better afterwards.

MONDAY, 24TH. The morning very cold indeed, strong wind from northwest. At 8:25 we continued our journey and traveled over level prairie ten miles, then halted to feed at 12:45. The bluffs on the north about two miles from us and the river one mile. About noon the weather began to moderate and grow warmer. While we were resting two Indians came to camp, their object evidently being to get the dog which has followed us to this place. They tarried a little while and then went away taking the dog with them. At 3:00 p.m. we again proceeded and traveled till 6:00 p.m., distance six and a half miles, during the day 16 1/2. Several of the horse teams gave out and they are evidently fail-ing but the oxen are gaining daily. The mules stand the journey well and in fact, all the teams considering the scarcity of grass. About 5:30 we discovered a party of Indians on the opposite side of the river mov-ing west. When we formed our encampment they crossed over the river. Some of the brethren went to meet them carrying a white flag with them. When the Indians saw the flag, some of them began to sing, and their chief held up a U.S. flag. It was soon ascertained that their object was to obtain something to eat. A number of them came to the camp and were conducted around by Colonels Markham and Rock-wood. They were shown a six and fifteen shooter also the cannon and the gunners went through the evolutions a number of times which seemed to please them much. They are all well dressed and very noble looking, some having good clean blankets, others nice robes artfully ornamented with beads and paintings. All had many ornaments on their clothing and ears, some had nice painted shells suspended from the ear. All appeared to be well armed with muskets. Their moccasins were indeed clean and beautiful. One had a pair of moccasins of a clear white, ornamented with beads, etc. They fit very tight to the foot. For cleanness and neatness, they will vie with the most tasteful whites. They are thirty-five in number, about half squaws and children. They are Sioux and have two recommends certifying as to their friendship, etc. The brethren contributed something to eat which was sent to them. Our course today has been nearly west, with a cool wind. The evening fine but cold enough to freeze clothing stiff when laid on the grass to dry. Elder Kimball has been quite unwell all day and mostly kept to his wagon. Opposite the camp on the south side the river is a very large rock very much resembling a castle of four stories high, but in a state of ruin. A little to the east a rock stands which looks like a fragment of a very thick wall. A few miles to the west Chimney Rock appears in full view. The scenery around is pleasant and romantic. After the Indians had viewed the camp, they returned to their horses and the rest of the party who have camped on the banks of the river about a quarter of a mile west of us. Elder Sherwood returned with them and soon after came back accompanied by the chief and his squaw who signified a wish to abide with our camp tonight. The brethren fixed up a tent for them to sleep under; Porter Rockwell made them some coffee, and they were furnished with some victuals. The old chief amused himself very much by looking at the moon through a telescope for as much as twenty minutes. Brother Fairbanks is much better this evening. Last night Luke Johnson discovered a very large petrified bone in the neighborhood of the bluffs as much as two feet wide, but he could not ascertain the length of it. After laboring sometime ineffectually to dig it up, he broke off two pieces and brought them to camp. They are very white and hard. It is now eleven o'clock. I have been writing in Elder Kimball's journal since dark, and have but little chance to write as much as I want in my own and his both, but I feel determined to do all I can to keep a journal of this expedition which will be interesting to my children in after days, and perhaps to many of the Saints. The evening is very fine but cool and I retire to rest with the feeling: 'God bless my dear family.'

TUESDAY, 25TH. The morning fine and very pleasant. Most of the Indians, men, women and children came early to camp on their ponies and marched around mostly trying to obtain something to eat. Several little barters were made with them for moccasins, skins, etc. John S. Higbee traded ponies with one of them. They have some good ponies and some inferior ones, but both males and females are neatly dressed and very tidy. They look cheerful and pleased to witness the camp, etc. At 8:20 we proceeded onward. After we started, the Indians left us and went over the river. One mile from where we started, we began to ascend a low range of bluffs to avoid a large, high sandy ridge which projects to the river. We traveled three quarters of a mile and descended again to the level prairie. At 9:40 we halted to let the cattle and teams graze, the feed being good and plentiful, having traveled two and a half miles, mostly northwest around a bend of the river. The sun is very hot, the roads sandy and hard teaming. The river is probably three quarters of a mile wide here and on this side there are many small islands. At 11:15 continued our journey and traveled till half past one, distance four and three quarters miles over a very soft, wet, level prairie. We then halted to feed and rest our teams, as they have been hard drawn nearly all day. We have seen no game for several days except for a few antelope and hares. The buffalo appear to have left this region and in fact there are little signs of many having been here. The feed is poor, mostly last year's growth and very short. One of the hunters killed an antelope, which was brought to camp and divided to the captains of tens. At 3:00 p.m. we started again and traveled till a quarter to six, distance four and three quarters miles, and during the day twelve miles. For three miles of the first of this afternoon we had a good road, but the last part has been very wet and soft, numerous ponds of water standing all around caused by heavy rains. We have camped on a very wet spot, but feed being poor where it was drier, it was decided to stay for the benefit of the teams. Our course has been about northwest, very little wind and the day very warm. Chimney Rock shows very plain and appears not more than two miles distance but is no doubt five miles distance or over. Another antelope has been killed and brought in by the hunters. Elder Orson Pratt is taking an observation to ascertain the height of Chimney Rock. The evening was very pleasant and the brethren passed away their time till after nine o'clock dancing. Porter Rockwell shot the two antelope spoken of above. He also shot two wolves. Latitude six and a quarter miles back, 41° 41' 46".

WEDNESDAY, 26TH. The morning very fine and pleasant. I have spent the morning working on Dr. Richards' map. At eight o'clock continued on our journey. Elder Pratt taking observations to tell the distance our road lies from Chimney Rock. Yesterday morning Stephen Markham traded a mule which was foundered and unable to work to one of the Indians for a pony. They put him in the harness a little towards evening and again this morning. When crossing a very soft place the whipple tree unhitched and struck against his heels. He ran full gallop towards the head teams and twice through the line of wagons causing several teams, horses and oxen both, to spring from the road and run some distance before the men could stop them. After running nearly a mile some of the brethren caught the pony brought him back and put him to the wagon again without any accident, except a little injury to the harness. After traveling four and five-eights miles, we arrived at a point directly north of Chimney Rock which we ascertained by the compass, having traveled since it was first discovered 41 1/2 miles. We proceeded till twelve o'clock and halted to feed, having traveled seven and a quarter miles, a northwest course, the road very straight and hard excepting a few spots where the water stands caused by late heavy rains. We turned south a little to get grass as the higher prairie is barren, and scarcely any grass on it. Porter Rockwell has killed two antelope and John Brown one which were brought into camp and are being divided amongst the companies as usual. Elder Pratt found that Chimney Rock is 260 feet high from its base to its summit and the distance from our road at the nearest point three miles. The latitude at noon halt 41° 45' 58". At 2:25 resumed our journey making our road nearer the river than this morning. The road somewhat crooked but good traveling. After traveling five miles, turning directly south to avoid a bad slough and went a quarter of a mile and then formed our encampment at five o'clock on the banks of the river. The last quarter of a mile was not reckoned in the day's travel which exclusive of that is 12 1/4 miles, course north of northwest. The feed here is good and sufficient to fill our teams well. Joseph Hancock killed an antelope which was brought into camp and distributed. Soon after we camped, walked out to the bank of the river with Presidents Young and Kimball to read to them some of the minutes of the old council. We were joined by Dr. Richards and tarried till seven o'clock, at which time a heavy black cloud was fast approaching from the west and was soon followed by a strong wind and a little rain which lasted only a short time. The evening afterwards warm and pleasant though somewhat cloudy. Carloss Murray has been trying to rear the young eagle caught on Saturday. After stopping tonight, he put it under a wagon and a while afterwards the men ran the wagon back, one of the wheels ran over its head and killed it. I wrote in Heber's journal till half past ten and then went to rest.

THURSDAY, 27TH. The morning very fine. We have seen a number of romantic spots on our journey, but I consider our view this morning more sublime than any other. Chimney Rock lies southeast, opposite detached bluffs of various shapes and sizes. To the southwest, Scott's Bluffs look majestic and sublime. The prairie over which our route lies is very level and green as far as we can see. The bluffs on the north low, and about three miles distant. The scenery is truly delightful beyond imagination. I have finished making Dr. Richards' map to Chimney Rock. Elder Pratt has measured the width of the river at this place by the sextant and found it to be exactly 792 yards. At ten minutes to eight we continued our journey and traveled near the banks of the river till 11:45, being eight miles. The route very good, hard and good traveling, although a little crooked. Porter Rockwell has killed two antelope and Amasa Lyman one, which were brought to the wagons and distributed. There are some heavy thunder clouds in the south and west and a nice breeze from northeast. At two o'clock we continued our journey over the same kind of dry level prairie, keeping not far distant from the banks of the river and making a straight road. At the distance of four and an eighth miles passed the meridian of the north-ernmost peak of Scott's Bluffs being 19 3/4 miles from the meridian of Chimney Rock. These bluffs are very high, steep, and broken like many others, resembling ancient ruins. They are probably two miles from north to south extremity, but not very wide. We traveled till 4:45 and formed our encampment in a circle near the banks of the river which from this place seems to bend for some distance to the north, having traveled this afternoon five and three quarters miles and during the day thirteen and three quarters, mostly northwest. Elders Kimball and Woodruff pointed out the road this forenoon. Afternoon Elder Kimball rode with me in Johnson's wagon while I read some of his journal to him. The evening is very cold, wind northeast, and raining some. Feed is good and the camp generally well. Another antelope was brought in by the hunters. The latitude of the northernmost peak of Scott's Bluff 41° 50' 52".

Patty Bartlett Sessions's brief entries record the events of the second company that left Winter Quarters on June 5, 1847 and arrived in Salt Lake on September 24. She is well known as the "Mother of Mormon Midwifery." One of the nearly four thousand births she assisted with during her life is recorded in this diary excerpt.

Diary Entries: Monday, [July] 26– Sunday, August 1[, 1847]

Monday 26   start 7 oclock go 20 miles at noon water and bait [feeding the animals during a break]   a grove of ceder on the other side   saw the Indians on the other side   they stoped unloaded their ponys in the cedars   we pased over the hardest sand hill we have found   I drove my team   was not well   went a foot untill I could scarce stand   crosed many small creeks   camp on large one two rods wide. Br Spencer is a head   he started last night   went five miles   Br Rich came up

Tuesday 27   start 7 oclock   go 18 miles   in the forenoon Indi-ans came   some we have not seen before   a big chief among them   when we stoped to bait they came like bees   their loges were across the river   I drove into a mudhole   got stuck   put on more team   came out   camp near the river   kill a ratlesnake close to the waggon   thunders and lightens   hard rains some

Wednesday   28   go   18   miles   cross   many   water places   mudy   holes   pased over ground that was over flowed by the rain last night   but litle rain where we were   at noon baited on the last grass we found   till night   in the afternoon came up a dreadful wind   thunder lightning   a very litle rain where we were   on the other side of the river the ground was all aflood   we pased over sand bluffs in the wind the sand and gravel flew in our eyes so we could not see   at times we had to hold our waggon covers to keep them from bloing off   this is ruin bluffs   we camp on the Pioneers camp ground

Thursday 29   go 20 miles   at noon bait and water   at the river good feed   we are in sight of chimney rock bluff   of sand looking like a tower on the other side the river or an old courthouse go over the blufs   camp   on   the   river   go   and   lay   hands   on   Mary   Jane Tomson   we have traveled to day behind Br Spencer   we came up with him last night

Friday   30   go 20 miles   pass the chimney rock   many places that looked like ancient buildings camp on the river   find good feed   kill a ratle snake   save the gall and greace

Saturday 31 -   go 15 miles   camp on the river   no wood and poor feed   the bluff on the other side looks like the temple   last night Brown & others went over the river on to the bluff   kiled 3 antalopes   a very curious looking place   the bluffs look like ancient edifices   some have gone over to night   we met Br Devenport this morning from the Pioneers   it gladened my heart to see him   he was in co with men that had been to Oregon   two women with them

Sunday   August 1   I was caled to sister Covington   I went back 5 miles   she came back with me   I put her to bed this evening with a daughter   P G Mary & Martha went over on the Bluffs   got 6 quarts of black curant   two catle died to day by eating a unfit substance that lay on the ground

Frederick Piercy was hired as an artist by the Mormons in England to record his journey to Salt Lake City. Today his work would probably be considered to be part of a media or publicity campaign. His journal and art work with extensive notes by James Linforth, made his book, *Route from Liverpool to Great Salt Lake Valley,* an instant success for Mormons seeking their Zion. Much of his art work is used in the following pictorial section. He left Liverpool, England, on February 5, 1853, but his journey across the plains did not start until Thursday, June 9, from near the Winter Quarters. He arrived in Salt Lake City on August 9.

Diary Entries: Wednesday, July the 13th to Friday, July 22

Wednesday, the 13th.—In the guides there is a notice of a "Lone Tree." All through the journey the lone tree had been in my imagination until at last I had associated an interest, a sort of romantic idea, with it, which became quite exciting. I pictured to myself an old, weather-beaten, time-worn tree, standing in mournful solitude on a wide-spreading prairie, having to encounter alone the attacks of the elements, with no companion to share the storm, or help to break its fury.

I could imagine it on a cold winter's night with its arms bare of foliage, tossing them in sorrow in the wind, being desolate and alone. Even sunshine and refreshing showers must be melancholy pleasures to a lone tree, for do not they prolong its dreary isolation! I started off ahead of the company with the intention of making a complimentary and therefore careful sketch of this tree, but I could not find it. Some unpoetical and ruthless hand had cut it down, so my hopes were blighted and my occupation was gone. We passed Ash Hollow, which is on the south side of the Platte, where we could see an immense herd of buffalo, which good judges said could not number less than 10,000. Travelled about 18 miles and camped near Calm Creek.

Thursday, the 14th.—Travelled along the Platte bottom, over a heavy road, then by the edge of bluffs to Crab Creek, a distance of 17 miles. Camped amongst arrow grass, bad for sheep, and very disagreeable to every body having sensation.

Friday, the 15th.—Travelled over a pretty good road to Ancient Bluff Ruins, which are curious natural formations, resembling ruins, as their name implies. They are fit abodes for Indian ghosts and goblins. Camped where the road joins the river, about 20 miles from Crab Creek.

Saturday, the 16th.—Travelled 13 miles and camped on the Platte. Chimney Rock in sight all day, and Scott's Bluffs in the evening. Chimney Rock is on the south side of the Platte, and on my journey home I made the accompanying sketch of it, engraved on steel, which is a view taken nearer by three miles than could be obtained from the north side. During the day I made a sketch of it from the west, represented by the wood-cut below. To the right of the rock the wagons are in corrall, which is the order in which they are arranged while camping. When danger is suddenly apprehended from Indians, the cattle are driven inside the corrall, but as the slightest noise from a dog, a wolf, and at times unaccountable circumstances, often cause a stampede, in which the cattle break down the wagons and rush madly from the camp, endangering the lives of the emigrants, frequently running until they are lost to their owners or fall dead, it is much the best way to tie them up to the wagons outside the corrall and picket them. In the latter method the cattle are safely guarded, and should Indians approach to drive them off or cause a stampede, they would be within range of a rifle shot all round.

Sunday, the 17th.—Travelled 6 miles, and camped on the bank of the Platte. Rain in the afternoon.

Monday, the 18th.—In the morning met 27 Elders from G.S.L. Valley on missions. They informed us that they had had a quick and an agreeable trip so far. We spent half an hour with them, and then separated, they to the rising and we to the setting of the sun. Scott's Bluffs were in view all day. They were certainly the most remarkable sight I had seen since I left England. Viewed from the distance at which I sketched them the shadows were of an intense blue, while the rock illuminated by the setting sun partook of its gold, making a beautiful harmony of colour. They present a very singular appearance, resembling ruined palaces, castellated towers, temples and monuments. In the foreground of the engraving are seen some emigrants hunting the buffalo.

Tuesday, the 19th.—Stopped to noon at Scott's Bluffs, and travelled about 4 miles to Spring Creek, making about 46 miles during the last 4 days.

Wednesday, the 20th.—Travelled over a pretty good road somewhat sandy in places. About 5 miles beyond is what is named Blue Rock. It is slightly grey, but by no means what may be called blue. Camped near the river.

Thursday, the 21st.—Saw Laramie's Peak this morning, which, by Elder Miller's account, was distant 75 miles to the south-west of camp ground. We travelled over a very sandy and difficult road. Visited a trading post kept by two Frenchmen, a few miles east of Raw Hide Creek. As the affair was made up of Frenchmen, Indians, squaws, horses, mules, oxen, dogs, trees, a shady bower, a sheep pen, a wagon, and a tent, it was most picturesque. Cattle in by no means good condition were from 90 to 100 dollars per yoke. I noticed that nearly all these trading posts were kept by Frenchmen, who were mostly married to Indian women. Camped on the bank of the Platte, 3 miles west of Raw Hide Creek. Travelled yesterday and to-day about 37 miles.

Friday, the 22nd.—Travelled about 9 miles over a good road to Laramie, and sketched what little I could see of it, but not having time to cross the river, I was unable to obtain a complete view of it until my return, when I made that which is used in this work. Travelled about 6 miles further, over a pretty good road, through rather a hilly country, quite different in character to that east of Laramie. Camped on the summit of a high bluff on the west side of a dry creek. I sketched Laramie's Peak, of which an engraving is given. Although its top was free from snow when I saw it, it is said to be generally covered with it, and that it 'acts the part of a condenser upon the vapour of the atmosphere which comes within its vicinity, generating clouds, which are precipitated in showers upon the surrounding country.'

PART III

Pictorial Journey

Artists

THERE ARE ONLY A VERY FEW ARTISTS OR PHOTOGRAPHERS SPECIFICALLY associated with only the Mormon Trail itself. There are, however, a number of other emigrant artists who sketched and painted scenes along the Oregon-California trails which include the major portions of the Mormon Trail. There are probably only two artists primarily associated with the Mormon Trail and familiar to Mormon Trail buffs. The first is Frederick Hawkins Piercy, a painter, who traveled from England to accompany a Mormon wagon company to Salt Lake City in 1853. The other is Carl C. A. Christensen who traveled over the Mormon Trail as a young man. He was a member of one of the handcart companies. However, it was not until almost twenty years later that he made his paintings. The paintings were meant as a chronicle of the history of the Mormon Church, and thus only a few depict the trail itself. There is a photographer, Charles R. Savage, who in 1866 left Salt Lake City by way of San Francisco, Panama, and New York to meet and accompany a Mormon wagon company and record its passage to Salt Lake City. Unfortunately, few trail scenes remain as many of the plates for his photographs were destroyed or have been lost. William Henry Jackson and George Simons were both recorders of the westward movement who sketched scenes along the Oregon-California trail systems that were used by the Mormons. The works of other emigrant artists, such as J. Goldsborough Bruff, James F. Wilkins, Albert Tracy, and Peter Hassen, are also used to depict the journey of the Mormons as they moved west to their new Zion in the Valley of the Great Salt Lake. The works of three artists, Piercy, Jackson, and Simons, comprise the largest portion of the pictorial section.

Most of Frederick H. Piercy's works included here first appeared in his *Route from Liverpool to Great Salt Lake Valley* published in 1855. It documents his trip to Salt Lake City in 1853. Piercy was born in Portsmouth, England, and by the age of eighteen had one of his paintings exhibited in the Royal Academy. His subjects were primarily portraits and landscapes. The Mormon Church had engaged in an extensive missionary effort in Europe, and by the early 1850s there were widespread conversions. The church was active in bringing its new converts to Utah. Piercy was engaged by the Mormons to travel and record their journey from England across the plains to the new Zion. Piercy himself did not convert to Mormonism but still accepted the position. He traveled to Salt Lake and then returned to England to have the narration of his journey printed. His route was a little different from the route in Clayton's guide. Piercy started his overland journey from Council Bluffs, generally following Clayton's north side route. He did not cross over to the south side of the Platte at Fort Laramie to follow the route as recommended by Clayton but remained on the north side of the Platte. Near present-day Casper the two routes rejoined, and Piercy again followed the original route the rest of the way to the Great Salt Lake. He made sketches of scenes both on his way west to Salt Lake and on his return trip. His works included not only major landmarks but also some of the sites having specific historic significance for the Mormons. They have become even more significant because the works of some other artists who travelled and sketched during the same period have either been lost or destroyed. Piercy's sketches were made into steel engravings or woodcuts. Some critics feel that while most of his work is accurate, some of his paintings are a little too idyllic or romanticized. Thus, notwithstanding the style of his work, it provides us today with one of the few "eyewitness" views of scenes along the trail. His narrative became a useful guide for Mormons and non-Mormons alike. He remained in England after his return and continued to paint. However, his paintings recording his trip to Salt Lake remain his most outstanding contribution to the field of history and art. His last art exhibit was in 1880. He died in 1891.

William Henry Jackson is one of the most famous recorders of scenes and events of the West. He was a photographer and a self-taught artist. In 1866 he decided to go west and signed on as a bullwacker on a freighting outfit heading for the Montana goldfields. En route he changed his mind and continued traveling west to Salt Lake City and then on to California. He returned from Los Angeles in 1867. During his journeys out and back he made many sketches of scenes and events encountered along the way. After he returned, he renewed his interest in photography, and in 1868, he opened a studio in Omaha, Nebraska. He began photographing the westward expansion of the Union Pacific Railroad in 1869. Then, in 1870 he became the photographer for the Hayden Expedition. His photographs taken of the expedition, which included the Yellowstone area, were instrumental in having Yellowstone designated our first national park in 1872. Later he turned many of his sketches and his early photos of the West into paintings depicting the emigrants' migration west. He was born in 1843, the year before Prophet Joseph Smith was killed, and traveled west after most of the Mormons had already migrated. Yet, the scenes along the route had changed little. His interests in photography and painting continued until he died in 1943 at the age of ninety-nine.

George Simons was another of the non-Mormon artists who captured scenes of the Mormons moving west and of the route they followed. He was a pioneer and a gold prospector in Colorado and hunted buffalo with the Indians. He travelled with his wife back and forth over the emigrant trails to California and served as a member of the railroad survey led by Grenville M. Dodge. He was also a poet and an artist. He made many of his sketches while traveling back and forth over the westward trails during the 1840s, 50s, and 60s. Many of his pencil sketches were also made into oil paintings. He was not a professional artist like Piercy nor a photographer like Jackson, yet his works are fine records of the time and events of that period. Like many other artists of that time, such as C. C. A. Christensen and James Wilkins, he also painted rolled panoramic views. His paintings were of scenes along the Missouri River and of the trail from Omaha west to Denver. Unfortunately, like those of some other recorders of the West, many of his paintings, including the panoramas and some sketches, have since disappeared.

PATTY BARTLETT SESSIONS—Daughters of Utah Pioneers

Patty Bartlett Sessions has been called the "Mother of Mormon Midwifery." During her lifetime she assisted in the birth of nearly four thousand babies. She was an early convert to Mormonism. She lived in Kirtland, Ohio and then moved west with the Mormon Church to Nauvoo, Illinois. She was a member of the first Mormon party to leave Nauvoo during the exodus in 1846. In 1847 she was a member of the second Mormon company that left Winter Quarters for Salt Lake. She was born in 1795 and died in 1892. She retired from being a midwife in 1872 after a long and successful career. Part of her diary is included in the diary section.

Pictorial Journey

COME NOW AND FOLLOW ALONG ON A PICTORIAL JOURNEY WEST ON THE Mormon Trail to the Valley of the Great Salt Lake. View the journey through the art of early emigrants that captured their journey. See not only the major landmarks, but many minor sites and historic places. Then compare the sites they recorded with those of today as photographed by the author. Relive the experience and journey with them.

WAGON—Reproduction Today

Most Mormon emigrants used one of two major methods of transportation on the journey to Salt Lake City. Wagons pulled by oxen were used by the first wave of Mormons in 1847. Mules and horses were also used. In the 1860s, the "down and back" wagon companies organized by the Mormon Church were also pulled by oxen. The other method employed by many was the use of handcarts. Above and below are reproductions of the two major means used by the Mormon emigrants, the emigrant wagon and the handcart. The handcart was extensively used during the mid-1850s.

HANDCART—Reproduction Today

EMIGRANT & HIS WAGON—Nebraska State Historical Society

This old photo shows an emigrant at rest next to his wagon. Below is a recent photograph of the author next to his mode of transportation. As the emigrants used their wagons for their homes on wheels, so did the author and his family use their vehicle while researching the Mormon Trail.

AUTHOR AND CAR—Today

ROADOMETER—Reproduction Today

A major concern of the emigrants heading west was determining how far they had traveled. Below is a model of a roadometer, developed and used by the Mormons. A variety of models existed at the time. This one is on display at the LDS Church Museum at Salt Lake City.

Death was a common occurrence along the trail, yet very few Mormon graves have been identified. Just east of Scotts Bluff, Nebraska is the grave of Rebecca Winters. She died of cholera on August 15, 1852. Her grave was marked by a bent iron wagon tire. Her long forgotten grave was rediscovered years ago when workers were laying track. The Burlington Railroad resurveyed the route and moved the track a few feet south allowing the gravesite to remain undisturbed until recently. Her grave has now been moved a few hundred feet east to a small park still near the railroad tracks but in a place safer for travelers to view. This photo shows the grave in its original location just before it was relocated.

REBECCA WINTERS'S GRAVE—Today

**PRAIRIE STORM—Jackson, National Park Service,
Scotts Bluff National Monument**

One of the many dangers facing emigrants on their journey west was the occurrence of violent prairie storms. The thunder and lightning could scare the stock. The rain and hail could tear tents and wagon canvas. Streams and rivers could flood, making crossing them difficult or even forcing emigrants to wait a day or more for the levels to drop to allow safe fording. The road could be heavy with mud, causing the wagons and animals to become stuck. William Henry Jackson encountered a Mormon company enduring a terrible storm in eastern Nebraska in 1866. His depiction of this event is above.

On the other extreme was the terrible dust that wagon and emigrants had to endure. They complained about the dust being in their eyes, mouth, food, and every place imaginable. Below is a photo of the dust that was kicked up on a recent four-wheel drive outing of the Oregon-California Trails Association along the Hastings Cutoff and Mormon Trail west of Fort Bridger. Even after washing and vacuuming the author's car three times, some of the dust still remained in it.

DUST ON THE TRAIL—Today

PAWNEE CAMP—Jackson, Smithsonian Institution Photo #1249

The Mormons usually were on very good terms with the Indians. Their Winter Quarters were built on Indian lands. One of the tribes living in eastern Nebraska along the Platte and Loup rivers was the Pawnee. Jackson took this photo of the Pawnee camp on the Loup River. Many emigrants mentioned seeing and visiting abandoned Pawnee camps. In 1847 Patty Sessions wrote in her diary "we pass the Pawnee village to day it has been burnt by the Sues [Sioux]."

As the emigrants neared and then crossed the South Pass one of the Indian tribes encountered was the Shoshone. The Jackson photo below shows Chief Washakie's camp near the South Pass. The Shoshone were very helpful to most of the emigrants crossing the plains. It appears that Mormon emigrants tended to have less trouble with the Indians than other emigrants.

SHOSHONE CAMP—Jackson, Smithsonian Institution Photo #1667

Illinois

NAUVOO WELCOME CENTER (LDS)

Both the Church of Jesus Christ of Latter-day Saints and the Reorganized Church of Jesus Christ of Latter Day Saints have visitor centers in Nauvoo. Both have been active in restoring new life to old Nauvoo. Each center has fine displays and programs and should be visited. Many of the restored pioneer shops and homes are located near them.

JOSEPH SMITH HISTORIC CENTER (RLDS)

NAUVOO—From Piercy's *Route from Liverpool to Great Salt Lake Valley*

The Mormon exodus from Nauvoo began in 1846. Piercy did not visit Nauvoo until 1853. By then Nauvoo had been sold to the Icarians, a French utopian society. The town and the Temple had deteriorated. This is how Piercy saw Nauvoo, and he described it as follows: "The city is first seen from the top of a hill about two miles from Montrose. From this point the beauty of its situation is fully realized....It is the finest possible site for a city....The first objects I saw in approaching the city were the remains of what was once the Temple, situated on the high-est eminence of the city, and which, in the days of its prosperity must have been to it what the cap or top stone is to a building."

Here is a similar view of Nauvoo today. If you look closely to the right of the center of the photo, you will note the Nauvoo water tower. To the left of center is the steeple of The Holy Apostles-Sts. Peter and Paul Church. The water tower is situated only a block from the location of the Nauvoo Temple. The Temple was even taller than the water tower.

NAUVOO—Today

OLD NAUVOO—Courtesy Library-Archives of Reorganized Church of Jesus Christ of Latter Day Saints

This old daguerreotype of Nauvoo showing the Temple on the hill was taken from the southwest section of the city, probably taken in 1845, the year before its final completion and the beginning of the Mormon exodus in 1846.

Within a few years after the exodus of the Mormons, what was once the second largest city in Illinois, and one of the largest cities in the United States, had begun to deteriorate. Most of the old buildings don't exist today. Only a few of the buildings have been restored. Fortunately, many of the most historic buildings remain today. A close-up of the carriage house in the old photo is shown below. Today Mormon missionaries and volunteers are continuing to restore or reconstruct replicas of the original structures and conduct highly professional and friendly tours throughout old Nauvoo.

CARRIAGE HOUSE—Today

BRIGHAM YOUNG'S HOUSE—Hall, LDS Church Archives

This early engraving shows Brigham Young's home in old Nauvoo, which has been restored. After Joseph Smith died, many of the important meetings that helped to guide the Mormon Church took place in the room on the left of the outside door.

BRIGHAM YOUNG'S HOUSE—Today

HEBER KIMBALL'S HOME—Hall, LDS Church Archives

This engraving shows the home of Mormon leader Heber C. Kimball. Because of the growth of the trees around the building, the picture below was taken from the opposite side. The home is also open to visitors to tour. The roof of Kimball's home can also be seen in the old photo of Nauvoo on page 89, just below the Temple.

KIMBALL'S HOME—Today

JOSEPH SMITH'S HOME AND GRAVES—Today

Here is Joseph Smith's first home in Nauvoo. He bought the structure and lived there from 1839 to 1843. It is referred to as "the Homestead." The home was enlarged as is evident by the addition. In the foreground are the graves of Joseph Smith, his wife, Emma, and Hyrum Smith. "The Mansion," Smith's second home, which he built, is across the street. Both homes are open to the public.

This daguerreotype shows the Mormon Temple before it was completed in 1846. Even though the Mormons had agreed to leave Nauvoo, they still kept on working on their temple until it was completed.

NAUVOO TEMPLE—Utah State Historical Society

OLD STONE ARCHED BRIDGE—Today

This old bridge at one time carried the main road into Nauvoo. Today it is situated in a small park off the main road. You cannot drive over it, but you can walk on it. Think of all the historic figures and thousands of common people who used it coming to Nauvoo.

Below is a painting by C. C. A. Christensen depicting the route taken by many of the Mormons when they were forced to leave Nauvoo in 1846. Fortunately, the winter was so cold that for a short time the Mississippi River froze, and many of the Mormons were able to drive their wagons and teams safely across the ice.

**EXODUS FROM NAUVOO—Christensen,
Museum of Art, Brigham Young University**

93

DESTROYED TEMPLE—Piercy, LDS Church Archives

Piercy visited the site of the Nauvoo Temple. The Temple had been burned on October 10, 1848, and a few years later a storm blew much of it down. Shortly after Piercy made this drawing, the rest of the temple was torn down for safety reasons. Piercy had noted that the people who moved in after the Mormons left "have used the stones of the Temple to build workshops and a school-house."

Below is a view of the Temple site today. It was excavated in 1962. Only the outline foundation remains. The ruins of the baptismal well are also extant.

TEMPLE SITE—Today

CARTHAGE JAIL—Piercy, LDS Church Archives

Piercy visited the Carthage Jail, the site of the murders of Joseph and Hyrum Smith, in 1853, nine years after the event. Joseph and Hyrum were being held in jail awaiting trial on trumped up charges when a mob broke in, killed the two brothers, and critically wounded John Taylor. Only Willard Richards escaped serious harm. Joseph fell through the second floor center window on the left when he was shot. Piercy wrote, "I felt very anxious to visit Carthage...I considered that sketches of its jail would possess undying interest for tens of thousands, and concluded not to return without them." He was right!!

Here is the Carthage Jail today. The building functioned as a jail until 1866, after which time it was used only as a residence. It was acquired by the Mormon Church in 1903 and restored in 1939. It seems that only the well housing and the trees have changed.

CARTHAGE JAIL—Today

CARTHAGE JAIL ROOM—Piercy, LDS Church Archives

This is the room where Joseph and Hyrum Smith were shot and killed. Writing about his tour of the jail, Piercy recorded, "The keeper was away, and I was shown over it by a young girl. The holes in the wall by the bullets still remain unstopped. The bullet hole in the door is that made by the ball which caused the death of Hyrum. I was told that the stains of blood were still in the floor, but I could not see them, as the room was covered by a carpet.... After his brother Hyrum had been shot dead at his feet [while attempting to hold the door closed], and John Taylor wounded, Joseph attempted to leap from the window. He was shot [in the back] in doing so and fell through it, which drew the murderers from the interior, and gave Dr. Richards an opportunity to carry Elder Taylor into the inner prison and secrete him. Having seen the place and made my sketches, I was glad to leave."

Today the room looks much the same as it did then. Visitors can also see the bullet hole in the door from the ball that killed Hyrum Smith and see the window from which Joseph tried in vain to escape. Look closely at the door and you can see the bullet hole.

CARTHAGE ROOM—Today

Iowa

CAMP AT KEOKUK—From Piercy's *Route from Liverpool to Great Salt Lake Valley*

The Mormons with whom Piercy was traveling started their overland journey from Keokuk, Iowa, about twelve miles south-southwest of Nauvoo. Describing the Mormon camp he wrote, "I sallied out in search of the camp, which, after climbing a steep bluff on the edge of the River, I found most picturesquely situated on the top of a hill,...commanding a view of the country for miles around....The emigrants from each nation had wisely been placed together, and those who crossed the sea together were still associated as neighbours in Camp....Before leaving I made the accompanying sketch of the Camp.

Today Keokuk has grown and expanded over the area. Fine homes and a park stand where wagons once gathered and tents stood. This view shows a modern road that climbs the steep bluff at the edge of the river and follows the crest of the hill as shown in the sketch.

KEOKUK—Today

MT. PISGAH, IOWA—Hassen, LDS Church Archives

Peter Hassen made this drawing of the camp at Mt. Pisgah in 1846. This was the second of the major way stations set up by the Mormons on their exodus from Nauvoo. Garden Grove, farther east, was the first one developed. Small towns grew up at each location. They provided food and shelter for the emigrating Mormons. Mt. Pisgah was used by the Mormons from 1846-1852.

Here is a similar view of the area today. On the hill sloping from the left to the right are faint traces of what some think are remnants of one of the routes down the hill to the valley. There is a small park and a monument in the nearby cemetery with a sign commemorating the role this community played in the Mormon migrations.

MT. PISGAH—Today

PREPARING HANDCARTS—Spiegle, LDS Church Archives

Just west of Iowa City is Coralville. This was the site used by the Mormon handcart companies to outfit themselves after they disembarked from the trains that had brought them west. This engraving shows the Mormons hard at work building their handcarts. Today there is a small park in the area with different displays. One tells the story of the handcarts. Others deal with the geography of the site and the deaths that occurred. You can walk quietly through the area and imagine the sounds of all the emigrants working to prepare for the start of their journey.

HANDCART PARK—Today

FORT DES MOINES—Today

Farther west the Mormon handcart companies had to cross the Des Moines River. A number of the emigrants recorded seeing parts of old abandoned Fort Des Moines. Today this is all that is left. It is located next to the river near the crossing area.

Garden Grove was the site of the first way station built on April 25, 1846 after leaving Nauvoo. Very little archaeological work has been done here. Only recently has Garden Grove begun to receive the attention it deserves.

GARDEN GROVE—Today

MORMON CAMP NEAR PARK'S MILL—
Simons, Western Heritage Museum

There are very few illustrations of the Mormons crossing Iowa. Piercy did not travel with the Mormons once they left Keokuk. However, in the 1850s George Simons sketched and later painted a Mormon camp on Mosquito Creek just east of Council Bluffs (Kanesville) near the present-day Iowa School for the Deaf.

Today there is a marker and small display in the area on land adjacent to the Iowa School for the Deaf near the intersection of highway 92 and US 275. This view is not from the marker but from the old railroad right-of-way west of the display. This whole area was used by the Mormons as a camping ground.

MOSQUITO CREEK—Today

Kanesville (now C Bluffs) 1849, looking North from corner of main st & first ave)

COUNCIL BLUFFS—Simons, Collections:
Council Bluffs Public Library

This Simons sketch of Kanesville (Council Bluffs) was made around 1849, a few years before Piercy made his drawing of the area. This view is looking north. The Mormons had begun to settle in this area, which they first called Miller's Hollow, in June of 1846 before crossing the Missouri a few miles farther up river, where they established Winter Quarters on the other side.

COUNCIL BLUFFS—Today

ENTRANCE TO KANESVILLE—Piercy, LDS Church Archives

After leaving Nauvoo and Keokuk, Piercy returned along the Mississippi River to St. Louis and then took a riverboat up the Missouri River to St. Joseph, Missouri. There he started overland to rejoin the Mormons in Kanesville. This is how Kanesville (Council Bluffs) looked as Piercy approached it.

Jackson made the painting below showing the tremendous bottleneck that occurred at major river crossings such as at Kanesville. This is probably the middle or lower ferry crossing. Some emigrants reported waiting at Kanesville as long as ten days before it was their turn to cross. Soon a number of ferries were in operation in the area of Council Bluffs, but they were not always reliable. Today the I-480 bridge over the Missouri River makes it possible to cross in only a few minutes.

KANESVILLE CROSSING—Jackson, National Park Service, Scotts Bluff National Monument

MORMON FERRY (Iowa side)—Piercy, LDS Church Archives

Piercy made this drawing of the Mormon Ferry, or upper ferry. It shows the view looking west across the Missouri River. His sketch shows a calm and peaceful setting, very different from Jackson's painting. Look just above and to the left of the two waiting wagons and you will see two wagons across the river climbing a hill. That was the location of the Winter Quarters, which was abandoned by the time Piercy arrived.

MORMON FERRY SITE
(Iowa Side)—Today

The Mormon ferry was located a little north of where the present I-680 or Mormon Bridge spans the Missouri River. Here is a similar view. The route into Florence from the Iowa side of the river was similar to the one shown in Piercy's sketch.

Nebraska

VIEW OF MISSOURI RIVER—Piercy, LDS Church Archives

This plate shows the view from what was left of Winter Quarters looking northeast towards the Mormon Ferry. In his narrative Piercy wrote that a cabin, the last remnant of Winter Quar- ters, was being burned when he arrived. Note a cabin burning to the right in this plate. The wagons shown climbing the hill on the trail coincide with the view from the Iowa side view.

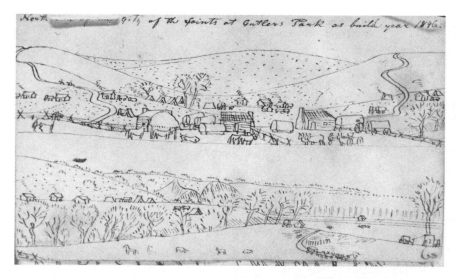

CUTLER'S PARK—Hassen, LDS Church Archives

This is another of Peter Hassen's 1846 drawings. The bottom half of the sketch is actually the right half of a panorama of the area. Cutler's Park was actually established before Winter Quarters. However, because of their concern for safety and their relations with the two local Indian tribes, the Mormons decided to abandon their camp at Cutler's Park and establish a new camp along the Missouri River near the ferry site.

Today there is a small marker in the area. It appears that the traces of the old road going up the hills as shown in the sketch are still evident. More trees have grown up along the creek, obscuring both the hills and recent construction in the area.

CUTLER'S PARK—Today

**WINTER QUARTERS—Christensen,
Brigham Young University Museum**

This is C.C.A. Christensen's painting of Winter Quarters. Note the cabins all lined up and the typical grid pattern used by the Mormons. A reconstruction of a similar log cabin is part of the Mormon Winter Quarters Visitors Center.

WINTER QUARTERS CABIN—Reconstruction Today

MORMON MILL—Today

Today two reminders of the Mormon past remain in Florence, site of Winter Quarters. First is the Mormon Mill, the only remaining Mormon structure. Turkey Creek, the stream that ran the mill, has been moved and routed underground. After the Mormons left, the mill was taken over and expanded. Years ago it was dismantled and then moved only a few hundred feet to its present site.

The second reminder is the Mormon cemetery. This memorial stands on top of the hill where many of the Mormons who perished that fateful winter of 1846-47 were buried. The statue depicts a mother and father bidding their final farewell to their young child whom they are burying in a shallow grave in the frozen ground. If you stand in the right spot on the right side facing the statue, you will even see a tear on the mother's face. This very moving bronze statue depicts both the suffering endured and the strength shown by the Mormons. None of the specific graves of the early Mormons is marked, but the names of more than three hundred are listed on a bronze plaque. The new Mormon Trail Center is nearby.

WINTER QUARTERS CEMETERY AND MEMORIAL—Today

steamer Omaha landing Mormons at Florence Neb in the Spring of 1854
Sketched by Simons

STEAMER *OMAHA* AT WINTER QUARTERS LANDING—Simons,
Collections: Council Bluffs Public Library

Within a few years after the Mormons settled the area steamers learned to navigate the Missouri River. This George Simons sketch shows the riverboat *Omaha* unloading Mormons at Florence (Winter Quarters).

Today the site is partially occupied by the water company. Part of the old landing area is thought to be near the right edge of the picture.

FLORENCE LANDING SITE—Today

Kansas

FORT LEAVENWORTH—James F. Wilkins, State Historical Society of Wisconsin, WHi(X32)20413

While Fort Leavenworth was not on the Mormon Trail, it did play a role in Mormon history. The Mormon Battalion came here for outfitting after leaving the Kanesville area. This fort was the location from which Kearny's army departed for Mexico and California in 1846. Note the blockhouse and trail going up the bluff to the left of center.

Below is a similar view today. You can walk up the hill in the same trail that the Mormon Battalion volunteers might have walked. Once at the top, only the base of the old blockhouse can be seen. The main parade grounds are only a short walk away. The Missouri River has now moved away from the bank shown in Wilkins's painting, but heavy rains still flood parts of the area occasionally.

FORT LEAVENWORTH—Today

Nebraska

ELK HORN FERRY—Simons, Collections:
Council Bluffs Public Library

The first major crossing for the Mormons and other emigrants after leaving the Omaha area was over the Elk Horn River. There were a couple of main crossing areas. Simons made these drawings of one site in 1854. The first one shows the view from the east side looking southwest at Mormon wagon companies camped and waiting for the ferry across the river.

Here is a similar view of the area today. The river has changed its course since Simons painted the site, but by examining the treeline and fields, the old riverbanks and course can be seen. Horses now graze where the Indian once sat.

ELK HORN SITE—Today

Ferry across ElkHorn River 3 miles N.W. of Omaha 1854

ELK HORN FERRY—Simons, Collections:
Council Bluffs Public Library

This view by Simons shows an actual ferry site seen from the west side looking back east at the approaching wagons. Possible remnants of the trail coming down the hill can be found and there are stories of possible graves in the area.

On Saturday, June 11, 1853, Piercy wrote, "The approach to Elk Horn is over a sideling road, and the descent into the lowland which borders the river is difficult. Another wagon was broken...." This is the view of the ferry in 1853 when Frederick Piercy came west with the Mor-

mons. He described the crossing, "On account of the narrowness of the stream they are able to stretch a rope across the river, which, being held by one or two of the ferrymen in the boat, by means of a smaller rope with a noose attached, enables them to guide the boat which is partly carried by the current, and partly dragged by them to the desired point on the opposite bank. The cattle were compelled to swim across." Here is Piercy's view of one of the ferries.

ELK HORN FERRY—Piercy, LDS Church Archives

Mormons crossing the plains with Hand carts from Florence neb to Salt Lake This train started from Iowa City and passed here Council Bluffs 1856

**HANDCART COMPANY—Simons, Collections:
Council Bluffs Public Library**

Simons made this sketch of one of the 1856 handcart companies. It had come across Iowa, had passed through Council Bluffs, and was then crossing Nebraska.

C. C. A. Christensen had been a member of a handcart company. This painting depicts the company turning out to rest as some of its members are crossing a small stream in Nebraska. The lady in the lower right can be seen gathering buffalo chips while people at the left are cooking. Where there was no wood, dried buffalo chips provided a hot smokeless fire.

HANDCART COMPANY—Christensen, LDS Church Art Museum

LOUP FERRY—Piercy, LDS Church Archives

Traveling farther west along the Platte River the emigrants came to the Loup River. They were sometimes forced to travel up the river for many miles before being able to cross it safely. While the river was comparatively shallow, it was known for its quicksand. The location where the vanguard party of Mormon Pioneers of 1847 crossed was different from places used in later years. Piercy made this drawing of the Loup Ferry near the mouth of the Loup in 1853. The drawing shows some wagons being pulled by mules.

The view below of the Loup River near the crossing shows how the area looks today. As with all the rivers in this area the flow has been greatly reduced due to the large amount of water taken out for irrigation.

LOUP RIVER—Today

114

**PAWNEE INDIAN CAMP—Jackson,
Smithsonian Institution Photo #1245-b**

One of the Indian tribes encountered by the emigrants along both the Platte and Loup rivers in eastern Nebraska was the Pawnee. Many of the emigrants had contact with members of this tribe. This 1870 Jackson photo is probably of one of the Pawnee camps along the Loup River. The Mormons met the Pawnee near this same area.

Simons also visited the Pawnee and recorded his experience. Today they are gone from the Platte River Valley. A lodge might have lasted about twenty years. A reconstructed Pawnee Indian earth lodge is one of the exhibits at the Stuhr Museum of the Prairie Pioneer.

**PAWNEE VILLAGE—Simons, Collections:
Council Bluffs Public Library**

BUFFALO STAMPEDE—Jackson, National Park Service, Scotts Bluff National Monument

Probably the animal that best symbolized the Great Plains was the buffalo. This Jackson painting shows a wagon company caught in a large herd while traveling along the Platte River. On Thursday, July 30, 1853, twenty-one days after leaving Winter Quarters, Frederick Piercy wrote, "I saw buffalo this day for the first time in my life. They are very singular in shape and run in a most grotesque manner, and apparently very rapidly. I had no chance of getting near them, but the enthusiasm of some of the hunters in camp drew them out in chase. I wish them success, for I was tired of bacon." Patty Sessions wrote on Friday, July 16, 1847, "see thousands of buffaloe...after we camped a herd of buffaloe ran in among our cattle."

Whereas buffalo were a common sight to the early emigrants from eastern Nebraska to the South Pass, some of the later emigrants rarely saw more than a few individuals near the trail. Today there are several buffalo associations concerned with increasing the number of buffalo again.

BUFFALO—Today

LASSOING THE STEERS—Simons, Collections:
Council Bluffs Public Library

One of the early morning activities was yoking up the oxen. Simons's sketch shows the scene of emigrants catching their oxen while camped along the Platte River. After they were roped the ox yokes had to be put on. For emigrants not used to this, it was quite a trying experience.

Here the oxen at Rock Creek Station, Nebraska, are being brought in after being lassoed. The Mormons who followed the trail from Independence, Fort Leavenworth, or St. Joseph would have passed through Rock Creek.

LASSOING THE OXEN—Today

LONE TREE
MARKER—Today

One of the experiences mentioned with enthusiasm by diarists along the trail was the sighting of trees. Most of the Platte River Valley was void of any big trees. Thus, seeing any large tree was a major event. This highway marker tells the story of one Lone Tree and its demise.

Below is the actual site of the tree and another tree that residents planted to replace it. So many trees are now found in the area that it is hard to imagine a lone tree on the prairie. The site is located southwest of Central City near the Platte River. Read Piercy's account in the diary section. It describes his similar experience at another Lone Tree which was located a few miles east of Ash Hollow.

LONE TREE SITE—Today

CAMP AT WOOD RIVER—From Piercy's *Route from Liverpool to Great Salt Lake Valley*

A few days later the Mormons came to Wood River. Piercy made this drawing of their camp on June 26, 1853. The painting shows a beautiful pastoral setting. I am sure that a few months later while crossing the deserts they must have looked back fondly at their camp on Wood River.

Here is a similar view of the area today along Wood River just south of Grand Island. The river is off in the trees on the right. Although the author found cattle grazing in the same area, they walked away and appear only as specks in the background.

WOOD RIVER AREA—Today

which brought us again close to the River (North Fork of Platte)

Outlet of Ash Hollow

In the river flat we found the ground coo

ASH HOLLOW—Jagger, California Historical Society

Ash Hollow marked one of the locations where those emigrants who had been following the Oregon Trail on the south side of the Platte River met the North Platte River. It served as a reference point for the Mormon vanguard pioneers in 1847. D. Jagger, a '49er, made this sketch of the outlet on his journey to California. The Mormons traveling with Piercy saw the site from the north side of the North Platte River, a half mile away. Piercy wrote on July 13, 1853,

"We passed Ash Hollow, which is on the south side of the Platte, where we could see an immense herd of buffalo, which good judges said could not number less than 10,000."

Here is a view of the mouth of Ash Hollow today. The course of the creek has been moved and channeled. For the emigrants who followed the early Oregon Trail from Independence, Missouri, the drop into the head of Ash Hollow was steep and dangerous.

ASH HOLLOW OUTLET—Today

120

TRAIL REMAINS—Today

Two days after passing Ash Hollow, the Mormon Trail approached "Ancient Bluff Ruins." The trail along the Platte River was often very wide. This view shows the width of the trail a few miles east of Ancient Bluffs Ruins just off Highway 26 as the trail approaches what Clayton called "high bluffs," known today as Indian Lookout Point. Very often parallel paths were cut into the plains.

This is a view of the famous "Ancient Bluff Ruins" just to the north of the present-day Highways 26 and 92 west of Lisco. It was first named "Bluff Ruins" by Dr. Richards, who was traveling with the 1847 Pioneer Company when they camped there. Later Mormon companies frequently camped in the area and climbed the bluff as members of the Pioneer Company had. Hariett Buckingham wrote in 1851 "...climbed the highest ruin which commanded a fine view of the country....we left our names upon a Buffalo bone which lay bleaching on the top from the river it presents the appearance of a fortified city falling to decay, but the nearer you draw nigh the illusion vanishes."

ANCIENT BLUFF RUINS—Today

COURTHOUSE AND JAIL ROCKS—Bruff, Yale Collection of Western Americana, Beinecke Rare Book and Manuscript Library

While these two landmarks were not on the Mormon Trail on the north side of the North Platte River, they could be seen by the Mormons. Clayton's guide had earlier noted, "Castle Bluffs, south side the river" referring to the various interesting land formations west of Ash Hollow for the next eighty miles to Scotts Bluff.

Some may even have thought that this was Chimney Rock. For the Mormons who travelled on the south side this was the view they would have seen. Those on the north side had a more distant view.

Here is a similar view of the same area today.

COURTHOUSE AND JAIL ROCKS—Today

CHIMNEY ROCK—Piercy, Nebraska State Historical Society

This is one of two drawings of Chimney Rock by Piercy. Writing in his journal he noted, "Travelled 13 miles and camped on the Platte, Chimney Rock in sight all day, and Scott's Bluffs in the evening. Chimney Rock is on the south side of the Platte, and on my journey home I made the accompanying sketch of it...which is taken nearer by three miles than it could be obtained from the north side." Some Mormons first reported seeing what they thought was Chimney Rock by climbing some bluffs two miles west of present-day Lisco, Nebraska.

Here is a view similar to Piercy's. Of all the landmarks on all the emigrant trails, Chimney Rock is the one most frequently mentioned in diaries. Lucy Canfield, a Mormon emigrant, camped opposite Chimney Rock September 1, 1862 and wrote, "Tis a wild and romantic country around this rock." It still is today. Wagon train rides are available in the area.

CHIMNEY ROCK—Today

**SCOTTS BLUFF—From Piercy's *Route
from Liverpool to Great Salt Lake Valley***

Piercy noted in his journal, "Scott's Bluffs were in view all day. They were certainly the most remarkable sight I had seen since I left England. Viewed from the distance at which I sketched them the shadows were of an intense blue, while the rock illuminated by the setting sun partook of its gold, making a beautiful harmony of colour. They present a very singular appearance, resembling ruined palaces, castellated towers, temples and monuments."

Today the buffalo are gone from the area and tall corn grows where the prairie grasses grew. Here is a view from near the same location.

SCOTTS BLUFF—Today

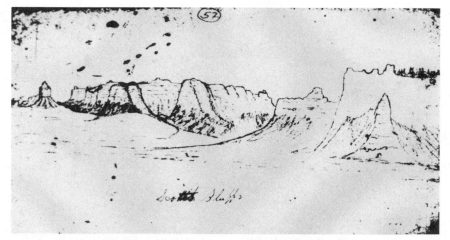

SCOTTS BLUFF—Simons, From Merrill Mattes's *The Great Platte River Road,* Nebraska State Historical Society

Simon's view of Scotts Bluff is from a few miles closer to it. His sketch is more basic than Piercy's drawing. However it is still possible to point out specific parts. Notice Dome Rock at the left, then the main south bluff, and the north bluff including the portion known today as the "saddle."

Here is a similar view of the area today from the north side of the river. This is the view the Mormons and other emigrants on the north side had. It is about one mile west of Rebecca Winters's grave.

SCOTTS BLUFF—Today

Wyoming

CROSSING THE NORTH PLATTE—Christensen, Museum of Art, Brigham Young University

This C. C. A. Christensen painting depicts the Mormon vanguard pioneer party breaking camp and then crossing the Platte River.

Charles Savage took this photo of a Mormon wagon company crossing the Platte River in August 1866. There were no trees in sight where this company crossed the river. Another part of the wagon company is barely visible in the distant background.

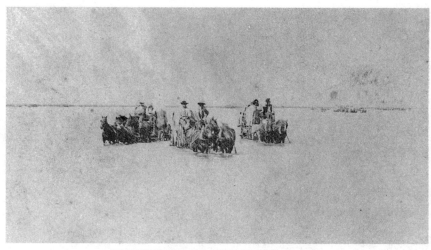

CROSSING THE PLATTE RIVER—Savage, Nebraska State Historical Society

FORT LARAMIE—From Piercy's *Route from Liverpool to Great Salt Lake Valley*

Piercy visited and sketched the fort twice, first on his way out and then again on his return. This view was made during his return trip. It shows both the old adobe Fort John (also known as Fort Laramie) and the rapidly expanding military construction of the new Fort Laramie.

Here is a similar view. Old Fort John has been replaced. However, Old Bedlam, the officers' quarters is still standing. Trees have grown up along the river bank and the river has changed its course a little making it impossible to duplicate the exact scene.

FORT LARAMIE—Today

LARAMIE PEAK—From Piercy's *Route from Liverpool to Great Salt Lake Valley*

West of Scotts Bluff the Mormons could see Laramie Peak dominating the western horizon. This sketch was made a few miles west of Fort Laramie. Laramie Peak would be in view for the next 100 miles. Piercy wrote, "Camped on the summit of a high bluff on the west side of a dry creek. I sketched Laramie Peak...." At this point Piercy was still traveling on the north side of the river on what has been called the Chiles Route. The view is from near where the trail turned north a few miles east of Guernsey. The early Mormon companies had crossed to the south side of the river and were following the main Oregon-California Trail.

LARAMIE PEAK—Today

MEXICAN HILL— Today

Just west of Fort Laramie the main trail followed the bluffs. After a few miles it dropped off the bluffs to the river and within a few more miles it had to climb back up over some hills. Clayton's guide records, "Steep hill to descend. The descent being over rock, and very steep, makes it dangerous to wagons, but it is not lengthy." This steep hill is known today as Mexican Hill. This view is looking back up the bluff in the cut made by the thousands of wagons that came down it. Just as Clayton said, it is very steep and narrow and, luckily, not very long.

Once in the bottom the trail was forced close to the cliffs. Then the area opened up for a short distance. It was a natural stopping or camping area. The emigrants carved their names all along the cliffs in this location, just south of Guernsey, Wyoming. The trail is in the depression from which the picture was taken. The cliff to the left is called Register Cliff.

REGISTER CLIFF—Today

129

DEEP RUT HILL—Today

Clayton's guide records, "Steep hill to ascend and descend. In traveling over this hill, you will find the road rocky in places, and about half way over there is a sudden turn in the road over rough rocks, which is dangerous to wagons, if care is not taken." The hill referred to is about one mile west of Register Cliff and is known as "Deep Rut Hill." The site is woven with trail ruts formed as the emigrant wagons negotiated their way over and around these rocks. Walk the area and you can easily imagine each wagon turning in one direction or another as the wagon in front of it was forced to pause because another might have broken down.

WARM SPRINGS—Today

Within a short distance the old trail turned south away from the North Platte River. One of the next sites the emigrants passed was "Warm Springs." Fremont had referred to these as "Emigrant's Washtub" because they were warm. Today the springs are still active, but they don't seem to be as warm as when the emigrants encountered them.

130

BLACK HILLS—Wilkins, State Historical Society of Wisconsin, WHi(X32)20438

James Wilkins made this painting of the area where one of the branches of the trail crossed Horseshoe Creek. It is perhaps one of his most accurate works.

Today trees have grown up along the creek bed. Interstate 25 cuts right next to the large butte today and crosses the creek in the general vicinity of the old crossing.

SIDLEY PEAK—Today

RED HILLS—Wilkins, State Historical Society of Wisconsin, WHi(X32)20437

Here is the trail as it approaches Wagon Hound Creek, about nine miles south of Douglas on Highway 94. The Mormon vanguard pioneers camped at La Bonte Creek. The next day William Clayton wrote in his journal, "At three and three-quarters miles passed over a branch of the La Bonte, a stream about ten feet wide but not deep. The descent and ascent being very steep, most of the teams required assistance to get up. For half a mile before we crossed this stream and three and a half miles after, our road lay over a kind of red earth or sand about the color of red precipitate. Most of the rocks and bluffs are of the same red color, only a deeper red. It affects my eyes much from its brightness and strange appearance."

This photo shows the same view. The wagons crossed the ridge in the center in a number of places. Note the erosion of one of those possible trail ruts in the foreground.

RED EARTH COUNTRY—Today

V. near La Bonté.

VIEW NEAR LABONTE—Courtesy *Omaha World-Herald* Quesenbury Sketchbook

These mountains with their distinctive curved and folded rock formations were subjects for a number of artists. James Wilkins and J. Goldsborough Bruff recorded them in 1849. In 1851 William Quesenbury made this sketch.

The view is actually much closer to the La Prele River than the LaBonte River. It was taken off Ayers Natural Bridge Road. The immediate area along the route of the old trail has not changed much. There is a small park nearby at Ayers Natural Bridge where modern travelers can picnic, wade in the river, or camp, much as some of the early emigrants did.

BLACK HILLS—Today

MORMON FERRY REPLICA

When the vanguard party of the Mormon pioneers reached the Upper Crossing of the North Platte in June 1847, the river was running deep and swift. There was no fort or bridge in the area. In order to facilitate a safe crossing, Brigham Young ordered a large ferry to be built. After a safe crossing, he named nine men to remain there to operate the ferry for the benefit of later arriving Mormons and also to provide a source of income for the Mormons. The site was commonly called the "Mormon Ferry." Within a few days the specific location of the ferry was changed. This is a replica of that ferry, on display in Fort Caspar, which was also constructed at the Upper Crossing.

FORT CASPAR—Jackson, Harold Warp's
Pioneer Village, Minden, Nebraska

Louis Guinard built a trading post at the Upper Crossing, then built a bridge. Still later troops were stationed there. At first, the post was called Platte Bridge Station, but later it was renamed Fort Caspar after Lieutenant Caspar Collins who was killed on the north side of the river near the fort during an Indian engagement in 1865. This painting of the fort was made by Jackson.

Fort Caspar was reconstructed to reflect its later military period. A partial reconstruction of the bridge was built on its original site. Some of the mounds left from the rotting piles and cages from the original bridge can still be seen. Jackson painted a view near the one below.

FORT CASPAR—Today

135

ROCK AVENUE FROM THE N.—Courtesy *Omaho World-Herald*
Quesenbury Sketchbook

After crossing the North Platte River the trail left the river to cut across to the Sweetwater River Valley. One of the geological features along the trail was Rock Avenue. Clayton's guide notes, "Rock avenue and steep descent. The road here passes between high rocks, forming a kind of avenue or gateway for a quarter mile." Sohia Goodridge may have had Clayton's guide as she recorded on September 5, 1850, "We came through a place called Rock Avenue. It is about a quarter of a mile long and lined with rocks on each side." On August 11, 1863 Mary Lightner wrote, "Came to what is termed the 'Devil's Back Bone.' It consists of a long range of rock, and looks as though they were thrown up from beneath, and pointing up like ice in a jamb. It is a singular sight." J. Goldsborough Bruff made a sketch in 1849, and William Quesenbury made this similar one in 1851.

Recent widening and grading of the road has eliminated most of the old trail ruts in the immediate area, but some are still left on the north side of the present road as you enter the avenue from the east. Weathering of the rocks has now destroyed almost all of the names carved on the rocks. However, the view of the area is still the same.

ROCK AVENUE—Today

BUTTES ON THE SWEETWATER—Wilkins, State Historical Society of Wisconsin, WHi(X32)20444

Wilkins painted this view of the Sweetwater Valley after he had climbed Prospect Hill and started towards Independence Rock. William Quesenbury sketched a more accurate view of the area.

Here is the view taken west of the BLM display near the top of Prospect Hill. It seems very little has changed in this area since the emigrants traveled through here.

VIEW FROM NEAR PROSPECT HILLL—Today

**INDEPENDENCE ROCK—From Piercy's *Route*
*from Liverpool to Great Salt Lake Valley***

This is one of the most famous trail landmarks. Father Pierre DeSmet had called it the "great register of the desert." Piercy made this drawing from the southeast. He wrote, "We proceeded to the ford of the Sweetwater, about a mile beyond Rock Independence. Forded, and then, while the company was taking breakfast, I hurried back to the Rock and made a sketch of it. It is a large rounded mass of granite, on which are inscribed the names of many passing emigrants." Alfred J. Miller had painted it from a variety of directions in 1837. Bruff, Wilkins, Quesenbury, and Jackson also sketched it.

Emigrants wrote their names on the rock with whatever they had available—paint, tar, or chisels. Some of the old names can still be seen. Here is a similar view of the rock, but the river has meandered a little.

INDEPENDENCE ROCK—Today

INDEPENDENCE ROCK—Jackson, National Archives #57-HS-385

Jackson sketched, painted, and photographed this rock a number of times. The old trail split to go around both ends of the rock. This 1870 photograph shows the trail on the north side of the rock.

Here is the same view today from the highway rest area occupying the site. A pedestrian walkway crosses the actual swale shown in Jackson's photo. For modern trail travelers a short walk and climb will bring you to the top of the rock. The view is well worth it.

INDEPENDENCE ROCK—Today

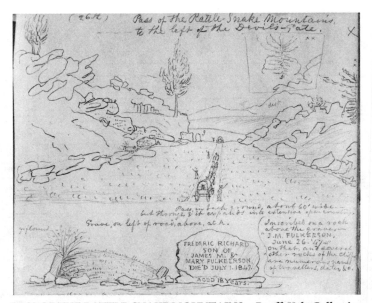

PASS OF THE RATTLE-SNAKE MOUNTAINS—Bruff, Yale Collection of Western Americana, Beinecke Rare Book and Manuscript Library

After leaving Independence Rock the trail headed west towards Devil's Gate. The trail did not pass through it but through a notch in the hills a little south of the gate. In 1849 Bruff made this drawing of the pass and Frederick Richard Fulkerson's 1847 grave. The Mormon Pioneer Party had passed here on June 21, 1847, ten days before Fulkerson's death. Later Mormon companies would have seen the fresh grave.

Here is how the pass looks today. Not much has changed. The grave shown in the sketch is still there, but the inscription is gone. In 1864 another emigrant, T.P. Baker, carved his name on it. Today the modern highway does not follow the paved road that was built on top or next to the old trail, but loops around farther south.

RATTLESNAKE PASS—Today

140

**DEVIL'S GATE—Jackson, Harold Warp's
Pioneer Village, Minden, Nebraska**

Jackson's painting captures the emigrants after they have passed through what Bruff called Rattle-snake Pass. Clayton wrote in his journal, "the road passes between two high ridges of granite, leaving a surface of about two rods of level ground on each side of the road. The road then bends to the west and a quarter mile farther, passes over a small creek...." Today the Sun Ranch occupies the site. The ranch road appears to coincide with the old trail.

DEVIL'S GATE—Today

DEVIL'S GATE—From Piercy's *Route from Liverpool to Great Salt Lake Valley*

Clayton's guide notes, "Devil's Gate. A little west from the road. The river here passes between perpendicular rocks, four hundred feet high—This is a curiosity worthy of a traveler's attention." It still is. Piercy wrote, "At Devil's Gate, about 4 miles further [from their camp near Independence Rock], I remained behind to make a sketch of this great curiosity, after which, as my boots were without toes, and admitted the gravel, which cut one's feet dreadfully, I had some difficulty catching up with the wagons."

Here is a similar view today. Unfortunately the steel plate copy of Piercy's drawing is not as detailed as his other ones. Jackson also photographed the area from a number of locations.

DEVIL'S GATE—Today

142

**SPLIT ROCK—Jackson, National Park Service,
Scotts Bluff National Monument**

Split Rock was another famous landmark. It could be seen to the west from Devil's Gate.

Alfred J. Miller painted it in 1837. At that time buffalo could be found up and down the valley. By the time the Mormons came buffalo were rarely found in the valley. This is Jackson's painting of the area.

Today the area looks much the same as it did when the emigrants passed through.

SPLIT ROCK—Today

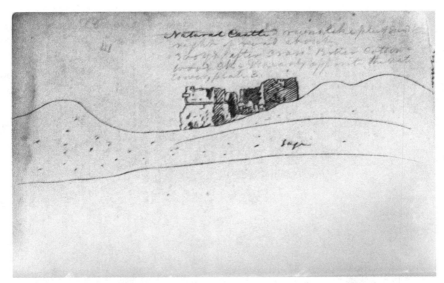

**SANDSTONE TOWER—Bruff, Yale Collection of Western Americana,
Benienke Rare Books and Manuscript Library**

This curious structure is on the south side of the old trail a few miles west of Split Rock. Bruff made this drawing of it. He, like many other emigrants, left the trail to examine it.

This is the view today of Old Castle. Only ranch fences are in the area. The old trail is now parallel to, or in a few spots, under the modern highway.

SANDSTONE TOWER—Today

ROCKY RIDGE—Wilkins, State Historical Society of Wisconsin, WHi(X32)20446

James Wilkins traveled to California in 1849, painting scenes along the way. This is his view of Rocky Ridge. The emigrants had been following along the banks of the Sweetwater, but near here the river entered a small canyon area. The trail had to cut over those hills. However, the tops of the hills were very rocky—thus the name "Rocky Ridge." Clayton's guide stated, "Rough, rocky ridges. Dangerous to wagons, and ought to be crossed with care." Piercy wrote "crossed rocky ridges very rough and tedious to get over." This is the only known early drawing of the area.

Today the view is the same, and the ridge can even be tough on 4x4 vehicles.

ROCKY RIDGE—Today

145

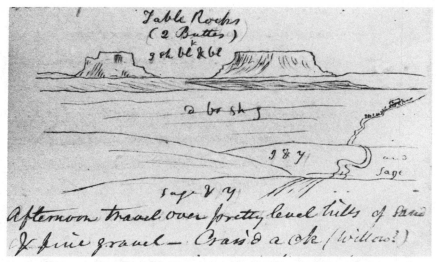

Table Rocks
(2 Buttes)
g rk bl & bl

a br sh j

g & y

sage

sage & y

Afternoon travel over pretty level hills of sand
& fine gravel — Crass'd a ck (willow?)

OREGON BUTTES/TABLE ROCKS—Bruff, Yale Collection of Western Americana, Beinecke Rare Book and Manuscript Library

These buttes marked the approach to the Great South Pass. They were in view for many days as the emigrants travelled along the Sweetwater towards South Pass. Their shape changed as the emigrants came closer and closer and then passed them. They were known by many names: Oregon Buttes, Twin Buttes, or Table Rocks. Jackson sketched them in 1866 and later painted them. Bruff also sketched them from a number of locations in 1849.

The view today has not changed much, only the trail is not as distinct.

OREGON BUTTES—Today

JIM BRIDGER—Kansas State Historical Society

Jim Bridger is probably the best known of the mountain men. He started working for William Ashley in 1822 as a trapper. For more than forty years he was actively involved in the history of the West. He was with one of the first parties to use the South Pass in 1824 and claimed to have discovered the Great Salt Lake. In 1842-43 he and his partner Louis Vasquez constructed a trading post, Fort Bridger, on the Black's Fork of the Green River. His fort was the starting point for the Hastings Cutoff. In 1847 he met with the Mormon pioneers and gave somewhat conflicting advice about the Salt Lake region. His relationship with the Mormons in that region was sometimes rocky. The Mormons purchased his trading post and strengthened it considerably. Eventually the fort was taken over by the U.S. Army. Bridger died in 1881 on his farm in Independence, Missouri.

SOUTH PASS—Wilkins, State Historical Society of Wisconsin, WHi(X32)20447

This painting appears to show the pass with the emigrant trail passing from left to right, east to west. The actual pass would be just off the painting to the right. It shows the approach to the pass and not the pass itself. Susan Noble traversed South Pass in 1847 and remembered, "We had heard so much of the South Pass that we thought, of course, a dangerous and difficult climb was before us. One can hardly imagine our surprised feeling when we found the Continental Divide as a long broad easy upland valley with splendid trails. It was hardly believeable...."

This is a similar view looking in a southerly direction. Pacific Springs is to the west of the pass. It was the first water west of the Continental Divide, and thus it drained to the Pacific.

SOUTH PASS—Today

148

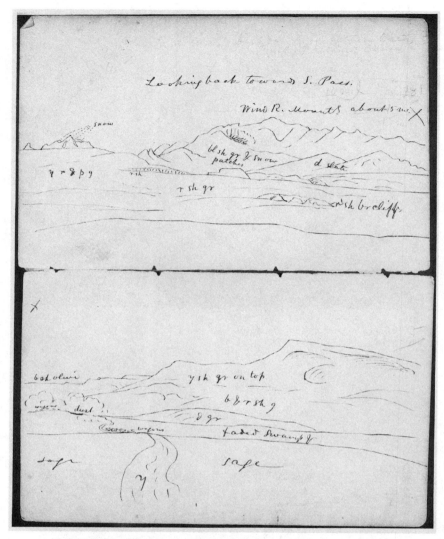

**SOUTH PASS—Bruff, Yale Collection of Western Americana,
Beinecke Rare Book and Manuscript Library**

Bruff made these sketches looking back east to the left and right of South Pass. Pacific Springs would be in the area labeled "wagons" and "dust."

Today there is a display area near where Bruff made his drawing.

LOOKING BACK AT SOUTH PASS—Today

**BIG SANDY—Jackson, National Park Service,
Scotts Bluff National Monument**

Jackson made this painting of the Big Sandy with the Wind River Mountains in the background. A few miles east of this area on the Little Sandy the Mormons met with Jim Bridger and discussed the Great Salt Lake Valley.

The painting seems to have been made from present-day Farson where the US 187 bridge crosses the river. For those modern travelers who would love some cold ice cream on a hot day, be sure to stop in Farson for a "Big Cone." West of Farson to the Green River the new road follows the old trail.

BIG SANDY AND FARSON—Today

FERRY AT GREEN RIVER—Wilkins, State Historical Society of Wisconsin, WHi(X32)20449

The Mormons crossed the Green River and established another ferry at the crossing. Later this area was called Lombard's Ferry. Crossing the Green could be very dangerous. Wilkins painted this view of the ferry across the Green River in 1849.

This is a view of the Lombard Ferry area today. The only difference seems to be in the width of the river. The Green has been dammed a few miles upriver and the flow is now controlled. The area is part of a bird sanctuary.

LOMBARD FERRY AREA—Today

**HANDCARTS—Jackson, National Park Service,
Scotts Bluff National Monument**

Jackson made this painting depicting the Mormon handcart companies that brought thousands of Mormons to Salt Lake during the 1850s.

This recent photo shows some Mormon students participating on a camping trip and religious retreat.

MORMON OUTING—Today

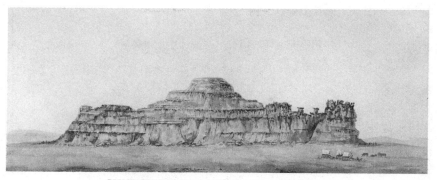

**CHURCH BUTTE—Wilkins, State Historical
Society of Wisconsin, WHi(X32)20451**

Clayton's guide makes no mention of Church Butte, or "Cathedral Rock," as Wilkins called it in 1849 when he painted this. In 1853, Piercy used neither name; however, he writes about it, "Just before arriving at Black's Fork, No. 3, where we camped, we passed a splendid range of clay bluffs which, as we passed them, seemed covered with figures in almost all attitudes— nuns confessing to priests, and warriors fighting, and transforming and varying themselves as we changed our position." On the T. H. Jefferson map it is labeled as "Castle Rock." There is an old story that one group of Mormons stopped for religious services at this rock one Sunday, and that might be why it was first called Church Butte.

CHURCH BUTTE—Today

155

CHURCH BUTTE—Jackson, National Archives #57-HS-462

Jackson passed Church Butte a number of times. This photo shows the rock looking east. Look closely and you will see a person at its base just to the left of center. Thomas Moran also drew the butte from the same location.

Below is the same view today. The author is standing in the same spot as the person in Jackson's picture. Little has changed in the immediate area, but there is a tremendous amount of oil drilling going on now—oh, what the emigrants walked over!

CHURCH BUTTE—Today

FORT BRIDGER—Jackson, Harold Warp's Pioneer Village, Minden, Nebraska

William H. Jackson first visited the then military fort in 1866 on his journey to California. This is his later painting depicting how Bridger's trading post looked in its early years. Bridger's post has been reconstructed very near to its original location. It was at this point that the early Oregon and California emigrants turned north to Fort Hall. Hastings had recommended that California-bound emigrants leave the Oregon Trail at Fort Bridger and head southwest on his cutoff. In 1846 Hastings succeeded in persuading a number of emigrants to take his new cutoff. The Donner-Reed Party was the last one to use it. When the Mormons, under the leadership of Brigham Young came to Fort Bridger, they were already committed to going to the Great Salt Lake Valley. They left Fort Bridger and followed most of the route used by the Donner-Reed Party.

Here is the reconstructed Fort Bridger. Be sure to visit this and take a step back in time.

FORT BRIDGER—Reconstruction Today

OLD FORT BRIDGER—From Piercy's *Route*
from Liverpool to Great Salt Lake Valley

After traveling about twenty miles farther from Church Butte the Mormons came in view of Fort Bridger. Bridger built this trading post with his partner Louis Vasquez hoping to capitalize on trade with the Indians, but more importantly with the emigrant trade. Piercy arrived there on Saturday, August 5, 1853, and wrote, "It is merely a trading post, then belonging to Major James Bridger, one of the oldest mountaineers in this region. The fort is built in the usual form of pickets, with lodging apartments opening into a hollow square. A high picket fence encloses a yard into which the animals of the establishment are driven for protection, both from wild beasts and Indians. The grass in the neighborhood was abundant, but about a mile and a half from the fort Mr. Bridger had erected a board, on which was written a request for emigrants to keep a mile away from the place." Bridger Butte is in the background.

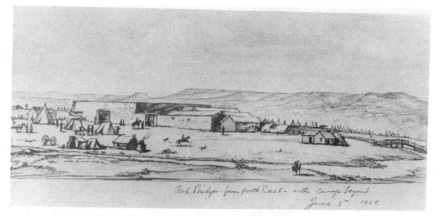

Fort Bridger from north East— with Camps beyond June 5" 1858.

MORMON FORT BRIDGER—Tracy, Utah State Historical Society

After the sale of Fort Bridger to the Mormons, Brigham Young had the old wooden fort strengthened. The fort was enlarged and a large stone wall was built surrounding it. Albert Tracy was part of the U.S. Army sent to Utah in 1859 during the period known as the Mormon War. When the Mormons withdrew because of the advancing U.S. Army, they burned part of the fort. Tracy made this sketch of the Mormon fort when the army took possession of it.

Below is part of the display near the museum. This part of the Mormon wall was reconstructed along the north side.

MORMON WALL—Today

159

ARCHAEOLOGICAL SITE—Today

The photo above shows archaeological work that has been going on for the past few years. The location of the base of the Mormon Fort Bridger is very evident with the wide rock foundation. One of the logs in the trench is believed to be part of Bridger's original fort.

Before the Mormons bought Bridger's post they had constructed a fort a few miles to the southwest, Fort Supply. Here a Mormon community existed and farmed the area, raising food to help supply Mormon emigrants migrating to Salt Lake. When the fear that the U. S. Army was going to invade and occupy the Salt Lake Valley grew, the Mormons were ordered to return to Salt Lake. The Mormons burned their fort at the same time that they burned part of Fort Bridger, which they had recently obtained. Today only a monument and some of the logposts remain in the fields that encompassed Fort Supply. Here are some of the logs at one of the corners where the blockhouse was. The fort was burned to the ground, but the constant freezing and thawing of the ground has slowly forced the remnants of the logposts up above ground level. The posts were originally sunk six feet into the ground.

MORMON FORT SUPPLY—Today

THE NEEDLES—Charles Savage, LDS Church Archives

The Needles were a major landmark on the trail west of Bridger's Butte. They marked the trail near where it crossed the Bear River and entered Utah. It was in this area that Brigham Young became sick and had to wait to recover before continuing west.

The view below is taken from the trail looking west towards the Needles.

THE NEEDLES—Today

Utah

CACHE CAVE—Today

Another major landmark is Cache Cave. Orson Pratt with the Mormon pioneers noted, "Here is the mouth of a curious cave in the centre of a coarse sandstone fronting to the south.... being about 8 feet high and 12 or 14 feet wide. We called it Reddin's Cave, a man by that name being one of the first in our company who visited it." Before the emigrants, it had been used by Indians and trappers. They cached goods in the cave,

hence its name. Clayton recorded it as Cache Cave. Today the area is closed to visitors. For years people have vandalized the owners' property and disobeyed their requests. It is too bad that many people have no respect for the rights of others. Please respect the owners' wishes.

The name of Mathew Ivory is carved on the wall of Cache Cave. A descendant, another Matthew Ivory, points to it.

CACHE CAVE SIGNATURES—Today

ECHO CANYON—Union Pacific Railroad

According to some, Bridger gave Echo Canyon its name. There is a tale that on Bridger's return trips to his fort from Salt Lake he would camp near the mouth of the canyon. Just before he retired for bed he would shout, "Time to get up, Jim." By dawn the echo would have bounced its way up and back down the canyon just in time to wake him! This photo was taken during the late 1860s when the Union Pacific was constructing the railroad down the canyon. Supply wagons are shown bringing equipment and materials. Soon the sounds of the iron horse were echoing throughout the canyon.

Below is the same area. The emigrant trail which was used to bring the supplies was later widened, graded, and blacktopped. Today the interstate carries most of the traffic, but travelers can still get off the interstate and take the old road to the mouth of Echo Canyon.

ECHO CANYON—Today

ECHO CANYON WAGON TRAIN—Charles William Carter, LDS Church Archives

This picture has often been used to show wagon trains coming down Echo Canyon bringing Mormons to Salt Lake City. However, it really shows one of the Mormon "down and back" wagon trains heading up Echo Canyon in the 1860s, on its way east to meet Mormon emigrants in the Omaha area and to bring them back to Utah.

Here is the same area today near Sawmill Canyon. The building of the railroad and, later, Interstate 80, changed the location of the stream. This is one of a few places in Echo Canyon where remnants of the old trail are still visible.

WAGON TRAIN SITE—Today

ECHO CANYON—Jackson, National Archives #57-HS-33

Jackson made a number of sketches and photographs of the Echo Canyon area during the 1860s, first, when he traveled down the canyon on his way to Salt Lake City and California, and later when the railroad was being constructed. This view is from the area known as the Amphitheater. It shows the old trail and the bed of the railroad that was being constructed.

This is the same area today. In his journal Clayton called the canyon "Red Fork Canyon" because of it's colored walls, but he also wrote about the echoes. Summarizing his experience there he wrote, "The echo, the high rocks to the north, high mountains on the south with the narrow ravine for a road, form a scenery at once romantic and more interesting than I have ever witnessed." All of what Clayton said is still true today.

ECHO CANYON—Today

**ECHO CANYON—Jackson, National Park
Service, Scotts Bluff National Monument**

Notice this Jackson painting of Echo Canyon. Jackson sometimes used earlier photographs for the basis of his later paintings. If the old photo was reversed, note how similar his painting would be to the reverse image.

Monument Rock is near the mouth of Echo Canyon on the north side of the canyon wall. Jackson took the below left photo in 1870.

Below to the right is the rock today. It seems that little has changed. The climb to the rock is steep.

**MONUMENT ROCK-ECHO
CANYON—Jackson, Colorado
Historical Society**

MONUMENT ROCK—Today

MONUMENT ROCK—Moran, from Bryant's Picturesque America

Thomas Moran painted this view of Monument Rock. Note the similarities with Jackson's photograph.

CAMP AT MOUTH OF ECHO CANYON—Utah State Historical Society

The mouth of Echo Canyon was a natural hub of activity. Here is a large Mormon wagon train. The early Mormons turned down Weber Canyon and then started their crossing of the Wasatch Mountains at present-day Henefer by following the Donners' route. By 1850 the Mormons had worked out a new route to Salt Lake City. It turned up Weber River and finally came out Parley's Canyon to the Salt Lake Valley. Except for about six miles, I-80 follows the route of the new Mormon road into Salt Lake City.

Today the site in the old picture is still a hub of activity. Interstates 80 and 84 intersect there. The railroad also emerges out of Echo Canyon at the same place.

CAMP SITE—Today

PARLEY PARKER PRATT—Daughters of Utah Pioneers

Parley Pratt was another of the early converts who joined the Mormon church in 1830. In 1835 he was selected as one of the Quorum of Twelve Apostles. He helped in the preparation of the exodus from Nauvoo in 1846. In 1847 he led one of the main companies to Salt Lake City. In 1849-50 he opened a new toll road through what is now known as Parley's Canyon. By 1862 that route from the mouth of Echo Canyon had become the main route into Salt Lake City.

WITCHES ROCKS—From Piercy's *Route from Liverpool to Great Salt Lake Valley*

One of the most interesting rock formations in the Weber River Valley is Witches Rocks. The site is located on the northeast side of the canyon. It seems that Piercy is responsible for giving the rock formations their name. On August 8, 1853, Piercy recorded, "We crossed Echo Creek from 15 to 20 times, most of the crossings were difficult. We passed many remarkable rocks to-day, but none I think so much so as Witches Bluffs, on the east bank of the Weber river. They are more like gigantic and somewhat rude pieces of statuary in the form of women than anything else. Out of compliment to their resemblance to the ladies I made a sketch of them." Thomas Moran also painted them a few times.

WITCHES ROCKS—
Today

Little appears to have changed. Some of the formations have eroded more.

WITCHES ROCKS—Tracy, Utah State Historical Society

When the U.S. Army passed through Echo Canyon and the Weber River Valley during the Mormon War, Captain Albert Tracy sketched the rocks from his camp.

**KANYON—From Piercy's *Route from Liverpool
to Great Salt Lake Valley***

After passing Witches Rocks the emigrant trail followed the Weber River and turned southwest at present-day Henefer to travel up Kanyon Creek in Main Canyon. This wood cut is based on one of Piercy's sketches. It appears to depict a view similar to one in Dixie Hollow. Heavy undergrowth of bushes and willows, along with the rocky creek bed, made travel very difficult and slow. The emigrants finally gave up traveling down the canyon and turned up Broad Hollow.

Below is a view of Dixie Hollow. The modern road has been cut into the hillside and fill covers up parts of the old route in the bottom. This view is located a short distance east of where the old trail turned out of Dixie Hollow and up Broad Hollow. Today the modern highway continues down the canyon, and there is a marker where the old trail turned up Broad Hollow.

DIXIE HOLLOW—Today

ENTRANCE TO SALT LAKE VALLEY—Hall, LDS Church Archives

This Charles Hall engraving of a H. L. A. Culmer sketch shows the first view of the valley the emigrants saw from Big Mountain Pass. The climb up the mountain had been difficult, but the route down was even worse. George Shep-ard noted, "went on down the longest and steepest and crookedest hill I ever see."

The area in the pass has been graded so modern travelers can park. The view you behold is the same the emigrants saw.

BIG MOUNTAIN PASS—Today

ENTRANCE TO SALT LAKE—Jackson, National Park Service, Scotts Bluff National Monument

Jackson made this painting depicting the emigrants as they came down Little Mountain and got their view of the Great Salt Lake Valley.

The picture below was taken near the spot where the emigrants came down the mountain into Emigration Canyon. This was the route opened by the Donners. The passage down the canyon was very difficult. Each succeeding emigrant company made the route a little better. It was the main route for the Mormons until the route down Parley's Canyon was developed in the 1850s.

EMIGRATION CANYON—Today

VIEW FROM DONNER HILL—H. L. A. Culmer, LDS Church Archives

This painting depicts a view looking west from Donner Hill. The Donner-Reed Party cut their way down Emigration Canyon. They finally gave up cutting through the thick underbrush and dismantled their wagons and hauled them up what is now called Donner Hill. The Mormons cut a road around the hill. This final section was their original contribution to the Mormon Trail. Clayton wrote, "While the brethren were cutting the road (around Donner Hill), I followed the old one to the top of the hill and on arriving there was much cheered by a handsome view of the Great Salt Lake....I sat down to contemplate and view the surrounding scenery. There is an extensive, beautiful, level looking valley from here to the lake which I should judge from the numerous deep green patches must be fertile and rich."

The picture below is taken from the balcony of one of the apartments that now occupy Donner Hill. "This is the Place" State Park is on the right in the near distance.

DONNER HILL—Today

175

GREAT SALT LAKE—Piercy, LDS Church Archives

Piercy created this drawing of the Great Salt Lake after leaving Emigration Canyon. He entered the Great Salt Lake Valley on August 9, 1853. He wrote, "Just before we turned the corner into the Valley we stopped at the creek, and having bathed and changed our clothing we entered as the sun was setting beyond the Great Salt Lake.... and another 5 miles brought us to the City." This is the view he had.

Below is how C.C.A. Christensen depicted the entrance of the Mormon pioneers into the Valley of the Great Salt Lake. The Mormon wagons are shown going around Donner Hill, which is to the left.

**ENTRANCE TO SALT LAKE VALLEY—Christensen, Museum of Art
Brigham Young University**

MORMON WAGONS—Carter, LDS Church Archives

This Charles William Carter photograph shows Mormon wagons in present-day Coalville. The route known as the Golden Pass Road down Parleys Canyon replaced the original route. It turned south up the Weber River instead of north down the river as the old road did.

Here is a view of Coalville today. The hills in the background give away the old photo's location.

COALVILLE—Today

PARLEY'S CANYON—Jackson, National Park Service, Scotts Bluff National Monument

Jackson shows the emigrant trail winding down Parley's Canyon. Parley Pratt had developed the wagon route down the canyon by 1850. However, it wasn't until 1862 that it became the preferred route for the entrance to Salt Lake City from Echo Canyon. Jackson first used the route in 1866 and then again in 1867 on his return trip.

Here is a similar view. Interstate 80 follows the "Golden Pass Road" as the route was known by 1850, into the city. Just around the mountain shown in the distant center the road opens to the valley. The floor of the canyon has been greatly altered by the construction of the interstate. Fill has been used to raise and flatten the floor, and sides of the canyon have been cut away to change what was once a narrow rocky gorge barely able to allow wagons to pass in some areas to a flat wide route for a six-lane interstate highway.

PARLEY'S CANYON—Today

SALT LAKE CITY, TEMPLE AND TABERNACLE—
LDS Church Archives

This is an early photo of Salt Lake City. The road on the left side of the photo is East Temple Street, known today as Main Street. It appears to have been taken from nearly the same place that was the basis for Piercy's drawing nearly two decades earlier, which is shown on the following pages. The Tabernacle appears to be completed, but construction on the Temple is not.

Here is a similar view of the area today.

SALT LAKE CITY—Today

179

SALT LAKE CITY—Piercy, LDS Church Archives

Piercy's view of Salt Lake City is looking south "from the 'Bench,' north of it, and just above Pres- ident H.C. Kimball's house, which is seen in t[h]e foreground, a little to the left of East Temple St."

MATHEW IVORY—George Ivory Family

Mathew Ivory was not one of the church leaders, but he was one of the Mormon emigrants selected to join the vanguard party of pioneers in 1847. He recorded his name on the walls of Cache Cave when they camped there. He entered the Valley of the Great Salt Lake on July 24, 1847. In August he returned east to help the main body of Mormons prepare for their journey west.

PART IV

Historic Sites

Museums and Displays

FOR THOSE WHO WISH TO FURTHER INCREASE THEIR UNDERSTANDING
and appreciation of the Mormon Trail experience, there are numerous
historic sites that can be visited. Many of these are conveniently located
along major highways; others are on smaller local roads. Most have
museums or displays that help tell the story of the trail. Some sites are
associated specifically with Mormon history, while others deal with the
experiences of all emigrants. Many will require hours to view and appreciate, while others have only small interpretive signs to read. All, however, represent historic events, places, or scenes experienced or viewed by
Mormons and recorded in their writings.

HISTORIC NAUVOO, ILLINOIS

This area is the natural place to start your journey back in time to the
1840s. Nauvoo had originally been built to be both the home and a
showplace for the growing Mormon faith. While today it is not the home
of the Mormon faith, much of it has been restored and reconstructed to
its original luster. This has been accomplished by the work of both the
Church of Jesus Christ of Latter-day Saints (LDS) and the Reorganized
Church of Jesus Christ of Latter Day Saints (RLDS).

Nauvoo was the center for the church from 1839–46. Here one can
find the homes of many of the famous early Mormons: Joseph Smith's
Homestead and Mansion House, Brigham Young's home, Heber C.
Kimball's home, plus many homes of lesser-known Mormons. Along
with these buildings one finds a wide variety of shops and businesses that
were typical of towns and cities of the mid-1800s: the blacksmith and
wagon shop, the carpenter's shop, the bakery, the printing office, the
post office, plus many more. One can take tours of the buildings, and
many of the shops have living history programs. On top of the hill, on

the grounds of the destroyed temple, there is a quiet park and a beautiful memorial. The graves of Joseph, Emma, and Hyrum Smith are also located in Nauvoo. Within the area are the Joseph Smith Historic Center (RLDS) and the Nauvoo Welcome Center (LDS). In addition to the tours and the displays and films within the visitor centers, there are also research facilities.

Historic Nauvoo is located in western Illinois on the east bank of the Mississippi River on State Highway 96, north of Hamilton.

CARTHAGE JAIL MUSEUM

This jail is the site of the murder and martyrdom of the Prophet Joseph Smith and his brother Hyrum on June 27, 1844. The jail has been restored to appear as it did in 1844. The small visitors center offers guided tours of the jail site.

The jail is located in the city of Carthage, Illinois, in western Illinois on U.S. Highway 136, about fourteen miles east of the Mississippi River. Nauvoo and Carthage should be seen together.

LOCUST CREEK CAMP SITE, IOWA

At present there is only a marker at this site. However, in terms of Mormon history, this is a significant site. It is where the words to the famous Mormon hymn "Come, Come, Ye Saints" were written by William Clayton. This hymn soon became the "Mormon Marseillaise." (See Wayne County Museum.) The hymn is reprinted at the front of this book.

The marker is located at the Tharp Cemetery off the main highways, on local roads about fifteen miles southeast of Corydon, Iowa.

WAYNE COUNTY HISTORICAL MUSEUM, CORYDON, IOWA

This fine county museum has a major display about the Mormon exodus from Nauvoo and across central Iowa. Here also is a display commemorating Clayton's writing of the Mormon hymn "Come, Come, Ye Saints." In addition to these Mormon-related displays there are other fine ones about the early settlement and life in Iowa.

The museum is located on State Highway 2 in the town of Corydon, Iowa.

Between Corydon and Council Bluffs there are some additional markers concerning two of the permanent supply camps and communities set up to assist other Mormons on their exodus from Nauvoo. One of the communities and markers is at Garden Grove Town Park, Garden Grove, Iowa, on Highway 204. A second marker is at the Mt. Pisgah

Historic Site near the town of Thayer, Iowa, on U.S. Highway 34. Ruts of the Mormon Trail may be seen near the Mormon Trail Park near Bridgewater, Iowa, and also in a field at Cold Spring County Park.

MORMON HANDCART PARK, CORALVILLE (IOWA CITY), IOWA

In the Iowa City area there are several markers dedicated to the handcart companies that left Iowa City in the 1850s. Iowa City was the end of the line for the railroad. Mormon immigrants from Europe and others who came by train from the East disembarked in Iowa City. It was in this area where the handcarts which were used by many of the Mormons on their journey west were constructed. Also in the vicinity is the small Heritage Museum. It has rotating displays depicting different aspects of the area's history.

Both the park and the museum are in Coralville, Iowa, off U.S. Highway 6.

FORT DES MOINES, DES MOINES, IOWA

The handcart companies crossing Iowa from Iowa City crossed the Des Moines River in Des Moines near the site of Fort Des Moines. The fort had been abandoned in 1846, but the ruins were still there when the Mormons crossed. Part of the old fort has been restored.

It is located near the intersection of Southwest First Street and Riverside Drive.

COUNCIL BLUFFS, IOWA

Within the area of Council Bluffs there are a number of sites related to Mormon history. This area was also known as Kanesville. It was named after Colonel Thomas L. Kane, who used his influence to try to help the Mormons during their persecutions. In this area were a number of ferries which crossed the Missouri River. This was the site of the Kanesville Tabernacle and the Grand Encampment, or the mustering in site for the Mormon Battalion, and some Mormon cemeteries from the exodus period can be found here.

Council Bluffs will also be the site of the new National Trails Center commemorating the significance of Kanesville in the migrations west.

WINTER QUARTERS, OMAHA AREA, NEBRASKA

This was the site that marked the end of the first portion of the Mormon Trail after leaving Nauvoo. Mormons ferried across the Missouri River and established their winter camp here in the fall of 1846. This became the famous "Winter Quarters" and was used as mile zero, the starting point for William Clayton's emigrant guide. Here is the new Mormon Trail Historic Center, the Mormon Mill, and the Mormon Pioneer Cemetery where many of the Mormons who died during the terrible winter of 1846–47 were buried. Displays include a reconstructed cabin and handcart. Today the cemetery's setting is beautiful and serene, and the statue commemorating the hardships endured at Winter Quarters is very moving. The Mormon Ferry was located by the site of the present-day Mormon Bridge (I-680), which crosses the Missouri River. Cutler's Park, another of the Mormon camps, is situated nearby. Unfortunately the mill is closed and deteriorating. The site has great potential as an educational and tourist attraction.

The new visitors center and cemetery are located in Florence, just south off I-680 before crossing the Mormon Bridge into Iowa. The Western Heritage Museum is also located in Omaha.

FORT LEAVENWORTH, LEAVENWORTH, KANSAS

Fort Leavenworth, Kansas, was established in 1827. It is still an active military post. Most of its history is not directly associated with the Mormon Trail. However, it served as the outfitting grounds for the Mormon Battalion in 1846. It was the assembly grounds for Colonel Stephen Kearny's command that marched overland along the Santa Fe Trail and the Gila route to California during the Mexican War. Few buildings are left from that Mormon period. The great swale of the trail coming up the hill from the river landing, part of the wall from the stone blockhouse, the Rookery, and the parade grounds can still be seen. The museum covers the complete history of Fort Leavenworth.

The fort is located off U.S. Highway 73, just north of present-day Leavenworth, Kansas.

INDEPENDENCE, MISSOURI, AND KANSAS CITY AREA

Within the Independence, Missouri, area are a number of sites related to the emigrant trails and the Mormon religion that are well worth visiting. One major museum is the National Frontier Trails Center. While its focus is on the Oregon, California, and Santa Fe Trails, much of the content here relates to the Mormon Trail since for much of its length, it coincided with parts of the Oregon and California Trails. The headquarters for the Oregon-California Trails Association is also located here.

Independence was a center of Mormon activity in the mid-1800s, and today it is the headquarters for the Reorganized Church of Jesus Christ of Latter Day Saints. The Temple and Auditorium are open for tours. The Mormon Visitor Center (Church of Jesus Christ of Latter-day Saints) focuses on the significance of the Missouri area in the history of the Mormon Church. There are numerous displays and programs available to visitors. There is also a Family History Center to assist people interested in researching their family genealogy. The historic Liberty Jail is located a few miles north of Independence.

Independence Square marks the beginning of the Oregon, California, and Santa Fe Trails and houses the Jackson County Historical Society and research archives. The mountain man Jim Bridger lived in Independence for a few years and is buried in the Mount Washington Cemetery. In addition to the items above there are many other historic sites, especially those related to President Harry S. Truman, who resided there.

There are very few major museums on the north side of the Platte dealing with the Mormon Trail. The Stuhr Museum is the exception.

STUHR MUSEUM OF THE PRAIRIE PIONEER, GRAND ISLAND, NEBRASKA

This is another fine musuem at which visitors could spend many hours. The museum has a wide variety of exhibits and buildings that cover the whole range of the history of Nebraska, including the Plains Indians, the emigrants, early road ranches, towns, railroads, and farming. A Pawnee Indian lodge much like those noted by Mormons and other emigrants as they passed through Nebraska can be visited.

The museum is located four miles north of I-80, at the junction of U.S. Highways 34 and 281.

MORMON ISLAND STATE RECREATION AREA, GRAND ISLAND, NEBRASKA

Modern travelers can camp along the Platte River near where the earlier Mormon emigrants camped. There is a small display and reconstructed handcart in the park. The recreation area is just north of the I-80 interchange with U.S. 34 and 281.

Seventy miles west of Grand Island in Lexington is the Dawson County Museum. It includes displays about the westward migration along the Platte.

The following museums are found on the south side of the Platte, off the Mormon Trail itself, but are worthy of visits. Most are related to sites that the Mormons on the north side of the Platte sometimes visited or looked for. All help to relate the story of the conditions on the journey west.

HASTINGS MUSEUM, HASTINGS, NEBRASKA

This museum is located away from the immediate vicinity of the trail but is another museum that has a lot to offer to the modern traveler trying to recapture earlier periods in history. Major displays focus on the American Indian, pioneer history, natural history, geology, early modes of transportation, firearms, and collectible Americana. In addition there is a discovery center for children, a planetarium, and a new IMAX theater. It offers something for everybody.

The museum is located in Hastings, 15 miles south of I-80 on U.S. Highway 281 at 14th Street.

FORT KEARNY STATE HISTORICAL PARK AND MUSEUM, NEBRASKA

This fort is a Nebraska State Historic Park. It was constructed in 1848, the year after the first wave of Mormon emigrants. It was first named Fort Childs, but shortly was renamed Fort Kearny. Today one can visit its fine museum, as well as the reconstructed blacksmith shop, magazine, and stockade. It is also possible to relax in the shade of trees which were absent when the emigrants first went west. The Mormons who left the jumping-off places of Independence, Westport, Fort Leavenworth, St. Joseph, or Nebraska City would all have passed Fort Kearny.

The fort is located about seven miles southeast of Kearney on L50A, off State Route 44.

NEBRASKA NATIONAL TRAILS MUSEUM (KEITH COUNTY), BRULE, NEBRASKA

This museum will commemorate the significance of the area at the forks of the Platte. Construction is under way for the development of a fine museum and exhibit area where the trails crossed the South Platte River. Plans involve the reconstruction of the old Beauvais Trading Post and Diamond Springs Pony Express Station and display of a working replica of an old Union Pacific train. Also featured will be the incorporation of the California Hill site where the Oregon–California Trail climbed the hills to the plateau to cross over to the North Platte. The museum will have displays focusing on the Indians, fur trade, the Oregon–California and Mormon Trails, the Pony Express, the Texas cattle trails, and the transcontinental railroad. Large bronze statues showing a trapper and Indians and two families, one traveling by ox and wagon and the other, a Mormon family, traveling by handcart are planned to lead you into the musuem.

The museum will be located near Brule, Nebraska, just off I-80.

ASH HOLLOW, LEWELLEN, NEBRASKA

This Nebraska State Historic Park marks the site where the Oregon–California Trails came down off the plateau to travel along the valley of the North Platte River. Brigham Young sent some Mormons across the river from the north side to verify his location. Today visitors can see the scars on the hills where the emigrant wagons dropped down into Ash Hollow. The area was a favorite camping ground for emigrants because of its fine spring, which is still flowing. A small cemetery is also located there. The museum has fine displays about the geology of the area, the use of the area by Indians, and the emigrant period.

The park is located on U.S.Highway 26, south of Lewellen, just after crossing the North Platte River.

ANCIENT BLUFF RUINS SITE, NEBRASKA

There is only a marker at this site. These landforms were often recorded by the Mormons and others traveling on the north side of the North Platte River. The bluffs were often thought to look like the ruins of an old fortress.

The marker and bluffs are located on the north side of U.S. Highway 26 near Broadwater, Nebraska.

COURTHOUSE AND JAIL ROCKS AND CHIMNEY ROCK STATE HISTORIC SITE, NEBRASKA

Chimney Rock is the most recorded landmark on the western trails. The early Mormons saw both landmarks from the north side of the river. Many strained their eyes hoping to be the first to see these sites. At that time there were no trees along the Platte to block their view. Today there is an outstanding museum at Chimney Rock, telling the story of the westward migrations. There are a number of hands-on exhibits that are terrific for children. Chimney Rock is also a National Historic Landmark.

Both landmarks are off Highway 92 near Bridgeport, Nebraska. Courthouse and Jail Rock are five miles south and Chimney Rock about fifteen miles west.

SCOTTS BLUFF NATIONAL MONUMENT AND OREGON TRAIL MUSEUM, GERING, NEBRASKA

The travelers on the north side of the river did not pass through either Robidoux Pass or Mitchell Pass at Scotts Bluff. However, the landmark was on the horizon for a number of days as the Mormons moved along the river. The Oregon Trail Museum is located at Mitchell Pass, which became the main route of the Oregon–California Trail in the early 1850s. Earlier trappers and emigrants used Robidoux Pass a few miles further to the southwest. The museum uses many of William Henry Jackson's paintings to tell the story of the migrations west. Visitors can walk in the path of the wagons that cut their way deep into the earth here. Some emigrants indicated they crossed the North Platte and climbed the bluff and had a spectacular view of the area. Today visitors may either walk or drive to the top of Scotts Bluff. The view today is still spectacular.

The museum is located on Highway 92 just west of Gering, Nebraska.

REBECCA WINTERS'S GRAVE SITE, SCOTTS BLUFF, NEBRASKA

While hundreds of Mormons perished on their way to Salt Lake Valley, very few Mormon graves have been identified. This grave is marked by a bent iron wagon wheel. After the survey the railroad relocated its tracks a few yards so as not to disturb the gravesite.

The since relocated grave can be found three miles east of Scotts Bluff just off U.S. Highway 26, near the railroad tracks in a park with a historical marker.

FORT LARAMIE NATIONAL HISTORIC SITE, FORT LARAMIE, WYOMING

The Mormon Trail crossed from the north side of the river to the south side, where it joined the main Oregon–California Trail. From here on emigrants to Oregon, California, or to Utah all traveled the same route. The first Fort Laramie, Fort William, was a wooden stockade fort, which had been replaced with an adobe fort, Fort John, when the Mormons first came through. The U.S. government soon replaced Fort John with its military structures. Today, it is the Fort Laramie of the military period that visitors see. This is an outstanding museum with many living history displays. The oldest structures are the restored Old Bedlam and the sutler's store. Within a few miles of the fort are many miles of trail ruts and swales as the Mormon–Oregon–California Trails traveled along the river.

The fort is located only three miles off U.S. Highway 26, west of the town of Fort Laramie.

REGISTER CLIFF AND OREGON TRAIL RUTS DISPLAY, GUERNSEY, WYOMING

In this area the wagons and handcarts were forced close to the cliffs and then over them. The wheels cut deeply into the ground and rocks, leaving dramatic evidence of the thousands who passed by here. Many people also wrote their names on the cliffs along the river. Today you can see some of their names and walk along the same route taken by those thousands of emigrants crossing the hill.

The sites are located at Guernsey, Wyoming, off U.S. Highway 26.

WYOMING PIONEER MEMORIAL MUSEUM, DOUGLAS, WYOMING

This is another fine example of a local community that has invested time and resources to develop an excellent museum. While its focus is not on the Mormon experience itself, one aspect is on the westward migrations. There are numerous other displays and fine exhibits which would be of interest to young and old—from the Indians to the range wars and to life in the early West— including guns, clothing, furniture, and many other items.

The museum is located in Douglas, off Center Street, in the Wyoming State Fairgrounds.

AYERS NATURAL BRIDGE PARK, WYOMING

This natural wonder was visited by many emigrants on their way west. There are no historic displays there, but there is a campground and picnic area. You may also wade in the stream, just as the pioneers did so many years ago. It provides a cool break and resting spot from the hot trail even today.

The park is located between Douglas and Casper, about five miles south of I-80 on Natural Bridge Road.

FORT CASPAR MUSEUM, CASPER, WYOMING

This is the site of the original Mormon Ferry established by Brigham Young in 1847. In 1849 another ferry was located a few miles down the river. Louis Guinard built a trading post and then a bridge over the Platte here at the site of the original Mormon Ferry in 1859. The military was stationed there in 1861. It was originally called the Platte River Bridge Station, and the post was expanded. After Lieutenant Caspar Collins was killed in 1865, the post was renamed in his honor. The fort was abandoned in 1867. The reconstructed fort holds fine displays about the trails west and a full-scale model of the Mormon Ferry. Other sites related to the last crossings of the Platte are also nearby. The site of the 1849 ferry and Reshaw's bridge are both within Casper. To the southwest is Bessemer Bend or the Red Buttes, the last area where emigrants, both Mormons and Gentiles alike, crossed the North Platte.

The fort and site of the 1847 Mormon Ferry are located in Casper on Fort Caspar Road just before it crosses the North Platte River.

HISTORIC TRAILS INTERPRETIVE CENTER, CASPER, WYOMING

Another museum in the planning stage, scheduled for completion by the late 1990s, is the Historic Trails Interpretive Center. It will focus on the different trails that funneled through Casper: the Oregon–California, the Mormon, the Bozeman, and the Bridger Trails. It will also include material about the Overland and Pony Express Trails, both of which went through southern Wyoming.

Between Fort Caspar and Fort Bridger there are no museums relating to the Mormon migrations. However, there are a number of sites and landmarks that were important to their journey west. Many of these are in the Sweetwater River Valley as the trail heads for the South Pass and can be seen from the highway.

INDEPENDENCE ROCK, DEVIL'S GATE, MARTIN'S COVE, AND SPLIT ROCK, WYOMING

These sites are all within a few miles of each other. Independence Rock was a major camping area. The Sweetwater River provided a large supply of freshwater and grass. The highway rest stop and display allow visitors to walk over the trail and visit the rock Father Pierre DeSmet had called the "Great Register of the Desert." Many of the names carved by the emigrants who passed by can still be seen on the rock. For those who have the time and energy to climb the rock, the view is beautiful, but be extra careful not to destroy the emigrant carvings.

The view to the west from Independence Rock shows Devil's Gate, where the Sweetwater River cut through the granite hills. The emigrant trail goes through a low spot to its south. Another display is located past Devil's Gate. The display deals with both Devil's Gate and the disaster that hit Captain Edward Martin's Handcart Company in freezing weather in 1856. Martin's Cove itself is about two miles west of Devil's Gate on the north side of the river. Looking further west one can see the famous Split Rock.

The display areas are located on Highway 220.

Additional landmarks the emigrants saw and wrote about can be seen further west along Highway 220 and U.S. Highway 287. Stops can be made at Split Rock and at the Ice Slough. The site of James G. Willie's handcart disaster of 1856, involving another company caught unprotected by cold winter weather, is located many miles off the modern Highway 28 and is difficult to find.

SOUTH PASS, WYOMING

This is the great pass through which emigrant traffic was funneled. Yet the climb was gentle and the pass wide. It was not a cleft in the Rocky Mountains as some people thought. Many emigrants might not have realized that they were passing through it if they had not been told where they were. The display tells about the signficance of the pass.

The interpretive site for the South Pass is about four miles west of the actual South Pass on the emigrant trail. It is located about forty-five miles southwest of Lander, Wyoming, on Highway 28. Looking back east at the pass one can easily see the green grass at Pacific Springs—the first water encountered flowing west to the Pacific. To visit the actual pass return east from the display area four and a half miles, turn south (right) onto a dirt road with a sign to the South Pass. Go about three miles and turn west (right) on the emigrant trail itself. Proceed one mile to the pass itself and the markers. Pacific Springs is two miles farther west on the rough road.

LOMBARD FERRY, WYOMING

This was the site of another Mormon ferry that was established by Brigham Young and the Mormon Pioneer Company in 1847. The Green River was, at times, a dangerous river to cross, and the Mormon ferry provided a safer passage for later arriving Mormons and other emigrants to use. Soon other non-Mormon ferries were established in the area. The display concerns the significance of this site.

The site is on the south side of the Green River where the Highway 28 bridge crosses the Green River.

CHURCH BUTTE, WYOMING

At present there is no display at the butte. The old marker has been vandalized. This landmark was sometimes referred to as Cathedral Rock, Solomon's Temple, or Castle Butte.

The butte is located on old U.S. Highway 30. Take the Church Butte exit from I-80 and head north and east about five miles on a rough gravel road.

FORT BRIDGER STATE HISTORIC SITE, FORT BRIDGER, WYOMING, AND FORT SUPPLY

Jim Bridger and Louis Vasquez established their trading post here in 1842–43. Many of the buildings from the military period of Fort Bridger have been restored and are open. There is a fine museum in what was once the infantry barracks. The Mormons who arrived in 1847 saw Bridger's log fort. A replica of it has been reconstructed on the grounds. There visitors can step back into the time of the mountain men. Also on the grounds is a small portion of a wall of the Mormon Fort, built after the Mormons had purchased the fort from Bridger and Vasquez. Extensive archaeological work is being done in the area. There are changing living history displays.

The Fort Bridger Historic Site is located at the west end of the little town of Fort Bridger off I- 80.

Another site southwest of Fort Bridger is the site of Fort Supply. Today there is only a marker in the tall grass next to a country road. However, in the fields are the remnants of some of the posts of the fort. Brigham Young had this fort built to provide supplies for emigrating Mormons, but also to act as a first line of defense. Modern travelers would have to inquire locally about directions to its location.

The next major museums and sites are located in the city of Salt Lake itself. However, while traveling down Echo Canyon in Utah travelers will again experience the same canyon walls and sights as the Mormons when they traveled. Within the canyon are some of the remains of the earthworks built by the Mormons as protection during the so-called Mormon, or Utah, War of 1857. No battles were fought during this "war." It was more a war of nerves.

SALT LAKE CITY AREA, UTAH

As the Mormons broke out of Emigration Canyon they had their first full view of the Valley of the Great Salt Lake and their "promised land."

Salt Lake City has many sites related to the Mormon Trail and Mormon history in general. The "This is the Place" monument and its beautiful sculptures, the Pioneer Trail State Park and Old Deseret Village with its extensive living history exhibits, Temple Square with the Temple and Tabernacle, the headquarters of the Church of Jesus Christ of Latter-day Saints (LDS), the Museum of Church History and Art, the Beehive House, the Family History Library, the Daughters of Utah Pioneers Museum, the Utah Historical Society Museum, and the Joseph Smith Memorial Building all deserve your time and attention in order to truly appreciate the Mormon Trail experience. Observe the layout of the city—its roads and parks even are related to early Mormon history. The city is basically laid out in a rectangular grid with streets wide enough for a wagon team to make a U-turn. Remnants of a low wall that surrounded the old city can still be seen. The Joseph Smith Memorial Building has an IMAX theater, showing a movie titled "Legacy," which highlights Mormon history, including the persecution, the martyrdom, and the migrations. All these are but a few of the things to see.

From Salt Lake City the Mormons soon spread out to establish new communities throughout the Great Basin area and into part of California. They played a major role in developing new roads and trails in the area—but that is another story.

PART V

Readings and Sources

Recommended Readings

FOR THE MODERN TRAVELER INTENT ON FURTHER INVESTIGATING THE
Mormon Trail there are a variety of books, both old and new, which are
available covering the myriad of topics related to the Mormon Trail
experience. Fortunately, some books that were out of print only a few
years ago are now available to the public. While some of the books mentioned are concerned with the general migration westward, most will
focus on some aspect of the Mormon Trail. This is but a sampling of
books available for the Mormon Trail enthusiast.

For the modern traveler there are a few books that can act as your
guide. Stanley Kimball is the author of many of these, among them his
*Historic Sites and Markers along the Mormon and Other Great Western
Trails.* Included in it are a series of thirty maps, detailing the major highways along with the Mormon Trail. The scale for many of the maps is
about eighteen miles to an inch. However, the range of the scale varies
from about eight miles to an inch to over sixty miles to an inch. Historic
sites are noted and a brief description is given about each. As the title
indicates, this book includes information about other trails as well. Some
of these other trails, however, such as the Mormon Battalion Route, are
related to Mormon history.

Another of Kimball's works, co-authored with Don R. Oscarson, is a
fine little book called *The Travelers' Guide to Historic Mormon America.*
Included in it are thirty-five site maps, pointing out the locations of a
variety of places that have played a significant role in Mormon history
since its beginning. These include sites in New England, the East, the
Midwest, and the West. Information about each site is also given.

There is another travel guide edited by Kimball. It is William Clayton's *The Latter-Day Saints Emigrants' Guide.* This is the book written in
1847 by Clayton for use by future Mormons on their journey to Salt Lake

City. Kimball's annotations allow the modern traveler to read not only Clayton's description of the route, but also what it refers to in relation to the modern highways. The guide starts at Winter Quarters and ends in Salt Lake City. There are five small maps which show the trail in relation to the modern roads.

LaMar Berrett is publishing two new books. His first, *The Mormon Trail, Fort Bridger to Salt Lake Valley,* is just the right book for following the route west from Fort Bridger. It includes all the useful material—large detailed maps showing the trail and significant site locations, including directions and other information about the trail—that make locating and following the trail easy. The second book is a two-volume edition in which he wrote some sections and edited the rest. One volume is *The Mormon Experience: Vermont to Illinois* and the second, *The Mormon Trail: Nauvoo to Salt Lake City.* These two volumes identify all the sites related to the development of both the Mormon Church and the Mormon movement west. Detailed site maps provide information never found in any other work.

Since the Mormon Trail overlapped much of the Oregon Trail, it is possible to use Oregon Trail books to examine parts of the Mormon route. Gregory Franzwa's books *The Oregon Trail Revisited* and *Maps of the Oregon Trail* are two fine books in this respect. As mentioned earlier, the Mormon Historic Pioneer Trail followed the Platte River on the north side but crossed the river at Fort Laramie and then followed the older Oregon Trail until Fort Bridger in western Wyoming. These two books will take the modern traveler mile by mile as they head west from Independence, Missouri. Aubrey Haines's book *Historic Sites along the Oregon Trail* lists and describes many of the sites the trails had in common. These three books will be very helpful. Also, since some Mormons themselves started in Independence, Missouri, these three books would cover that route except for the portion west of Fort Bridger. What remain to be published are books similar to these for the eastern part of the Mormon Trail from Nauvoo to Fort Laramie. LaMar Berrett's books, mentioned earlier, come very close to doing this.

There are a few books which I consider to be both classics and basic readers. One of the best of these books is Wallace Stegner's *The Gathering of Zion: The Story of the Mormon Trail.* This excellent book covers the story of the Mormons primarily from their time in Nauvoo just before their exodus to their arrival in Salt Lake. It also includes information about the influx of Mormon emigrants from Europe until 1869. Written in an easy, flowing manner, it is a must for anyone beginning to study Mormon history. For those seeking additional information concerning the handcart period, there is the book by Ann and LeRoy Hafen, *Handcarts to Zion: The Story of a Unique Western Migration, 1856–60*. This excellent volume provides the reader with a wealth of information about the Mormon handcart companies. It discusses the development of the idea of handcart travel, the Perpetual Emigration Fund, and the various handcart companies, as well as their songs and their journeys to Zion.

Frederick Hawkins Piercy's book *Route from Liverpool to Great Salt Lake Valley* is an excellent firsthand account of the journey over the Mormon Trail in 1853. Several of his drawings and diary excerpts are included in this book.

Mary Ann Hafen's *Recollections of a Handcart Pioneer of 1860* describes a woman's life in the Mormon frontier. She was a small child when she left Switzerland to come to Utah, and in this book she recounts her experience.

Another firsthand account is the reprint of William Clayton's *Journal* by the Daughters of Utah Pioneers. It traces the 1847 journey from Winter Quarters to Salt Lake, but omits the crossing of Iowa in 1846. For that information one has to find the 1921 edition of his journal.

Three other works should be mentioned. *I Walked to Zion* by Susan Madsen is a recent collection of short stories about the daily experiences of children on the Mormon Trail. The other two focus on the trails from Fort Bridger into Utah. The first is *West from Fort Bridger*, originally edited by Roderic Korns and Dale Morgan and recently updated by Will Bagley and Harold Schindler. This book follows the opening of the route in 1846 from Fort Bridger into the Salt Lake Valley and the routes across the Salt Lake Desert or north on the Salt Lake Cutoff. The journals of James Clyman, Edwin Bryant, Heinrich Lienhard, James F. Reed, plus related maps and waybills are identified and discussed. You can follow their progress as they helped to open the last segment of the route which the Mormons followed in 1847. The second book, *Trailing the Pioneers: A Guide to Utah's Emigrant Trails 1829–1869*, was edited by Peter DeLafosse. Included in it are some of the other trails used or opened by the Mormons in Utah. Small maps are included to help the traveler locate the routes today.

Then, of course, there are fine basic books about the westward migrations, such as Merrill Mattes's *The Great Platte River Road* and John Unruh's *The Plains Across*. Both of these provide the reader with excellent information about a wealth of topics. Mattes's book focuses on the Platte River corridor and the trails on both sides of the river. This is certainly one of the easiest books to read. Unruh's book deals with all the trails west and compares sections and examines different facets of the westward migration, including much information about the role of the Mormons. It is full of detailed information. Irene Paden's book *The Wake of the Prairie Schooner* and Bernard DeVoto's *1846: Year of Decision* are also two fine classics that cover the development of the westward trails.

For those of you who are interested in obtaining and reading more diaries written by women on all the trails, including many written about the Mormon Trail, there is Kenneth Holmes's *Covered Wagon Women*. These volumes cover approximately a fifty year period from the 1840s until the 1890s.

For those primarily interested in the Mormon Church and history there are James Allen's and Glen Leonard's *The Story of the Latter-Day Saints*, Leonard Arrington's *Brigham Young, American Moses*, and Dean Hughes's *The Mormon Church*. Allen and Leonard's book is one of the most recent and in-depth books written about the subject. Leonard Arrington's *Brigham Young, American Moses* is an excellent biography which examines not only his life but the various roles Young played in the development of Mormonism. It is full of information. For those seeking an introduction or basic overview of the Mormon Church and history there is Hughes's book. It focuses primarily on Mormon development during the nineteenth century with a small portion devoted to the twentieth century.

In addition to the works mentioned, one should always consult the bibliographies of all these books. This is especially true of Allen and Leonard's book which lists references by topic. Davis Bitton's *Guide to Mormon Diaries and Autobiographies* describes about three thousand items. Most of the museums along the trail have books available to the public that relate to the trail. Some are very specific or local in nature and can prove to be both very interesting and useful.

For now, happy reading! Happy traveling! See you on the trail!

Bibliography

BOOKS AND ARTICLES

Allen, James B., and Glen M. Leonard. *The Story of the Latter-Day Saints*. Salt Lake City: Deseret Book, 1992.

Arrington, Leonard J. *Brigham Young: American Moses*. New York: Alfred Knopf, 1985. Reprint, Urbana: University of Illinois Press, 1986.

Arrington, Leonard J., and Davis Bitton. *The Mormon Experience: A History of the Latter-Day Saints*. New York: Alfred Knopf, 1979.

Bagley, Will. "Lansford Warren Hastings, Scoundrel or Visionary?" *Overland Journal* 12.1 (1994): 12–26.

Berrett, LaMar. *The Mormon Trail, Fort Bridger to Salt Lake Valley*. Salt Lake City: Deseret Books, forthcoming.

Berrett, LaMar, ed. *The Mormon Experience: Vermont to Illinois, Vol. I; The Mormon Trail, Nauvoo to Salt Lake City, Vol. II*. Salt Lake City: Deseret Books, forthcoming.

Bitton, Davis, ed. *Guide to Mormon Diaries and Autobiographies*. Provo: Brigham Young University Press, 1977.

Brodie, Fawn M. *No Man Knows My History: The Life of Joseph Smith, the Mormon Prophet*. New York: Alfred Knopf, 1971.

Cannon, D. James, ed. *Centennial Caravan, Story of the 1947 Centennial Reenactment of the Original Mormon Trek*. Salt Lake City: The Sons of Utah Pioneers, 1948.

Carter, Kate B. *The Story of the Negro Pioneer*. Salt Lake City: Daughters of Utah Pioneers, 1965.

Commager, Henry Steele, ed. *The West: An Illustrated History*. New York: Exeter Books, 1984.

DeLafosse, Peter H., ed. *Trailing the Pioneers: A Guide to Utah's Emigrant Trails, 1829–1869*. Logan: Utah State University Press, with Utah Crossroads, Oregon–California Trails Association, 1994.

DeVoto, Bernard. *The Year of Decision, 1846*. Boston: Little, Brown, 1943.

Driggs, Howard R. *The Old West Speaks*. Englewood Cliffs, N.J.: Prentice-Hall, 1956.

Franzwa, Gregory. *Maps of the Oregon Trail*. Gerald, Mo.: Patrice Press, 1982.

Franzwa, Gregory. *The Oregon Trail Revisited*. Gerald, Mo.: Patrice Press, 1972.

Gowans, Fred R. *The Great Fur Trade Road: Discovery and Exploration, 1739–1843*. Orem, Utah: Mountain Grizzly Publications, 1994.

Gowans, Fred, and Eugene Campbell. *Fort Supply, Brigham Young's Green River Experiment*. Provo: Brigham Young University Publications, 1976.

Hafen, Ann W., and LeRoy C. Hafen. *Handcarts to Zion: The Story of a Unique Western Migration, 1856–1860*. Glendale, Calif.: Arthur Clark, 1960.

Haines, Aubrey. *Historic Sites along the Oregon Trail*. Gerald, Mo.: Patrice Press, 1981.

Hartley, William G. "Down-and-Back Wagon Trains: Travelers on the Mormon Trail in 1861." *Overland Journal* 11.4 (1993): 23–34.

Hill, William E. *The California Trail, Yesterday and Today*. Boise: Tamarack Books, 1993.

Hill, William E. *The Oregon Trail, Yesterday and Today*. Caldwell, Idaho: Caxton Printers, 1986.

Hughes, Dean. *The Mormon Church: A Basic History*. Salt Lake City: Deseret Book Company, 1986.

Hulmston, John K. "Mormon Immigration in the 1860s: The Story of the Church Trains." *Utah Historical Quarterly* 58.1 (1990): 32–48.

Jackson, Clarence S. *Picture Maker of the Old West, William H. Jackson*. New York: Bonanza Books, 1947.

Jackson, William H. *Time Exposure*. Tucson: Patrice Press, 1994.

Kimball, Stanley. *Historic Sites and Markers along the Mormon and Other Great Western Trails*. Urbana: University of Illinois Press, 1988.

Kimball, Stanley. *Historic Resource Study: Mormon Pioneer National Historic Trail*. Washington, D.C.: U.S. Department of the Interior, 1991.

Kimball, Stanley B., and Hal Knight. *111 Days to Zion*. Salt Lake City: Deseret News, 1978.

Kimball, Stanley, and Don R. Oscarson. *The Travelers' Guide to Historic Mormon America*. Salt Lake City: Bookcraft, 1993.

Launius, Roger D. *Joseph Smith III, Pragmatic Phophet.* Urbana: University of Illinois Press, 1988.

Mattes, Merrill J. *The Great Platte River Road: The Covered Wagon Mainline via Fort Kearny to Fort Laramie.* Lincoln: Nebraska State Historical Society, 1969.

Mattes, Merrill J. *Platte River Road Narratives.* Urbana: University of Illinois Press, 1988.

Paden, Irene D. *The Wake of the Prairie Schooner.* New York: Macmillan, 1943.

Sonne, Conway B. *Saints on the High Seas, A Maritime History of Mormon Migration: 1830–1890.* Salt Lake City: University of Utah Press, 1983.

Stegner, Wallace. *The Gathering of Zion: The Story of the Mormon Trail.* Salt Lake City: Westwater Press, 1981.

Stewart, George R. *The California Trail: An Epic with Many Heroes.* New York: McGraw-Hill, 1962.

Unruh, John. *The Plains Across: The Overland Emigrants and the Trans-Mississippi West, 1840–60.* Urbana: University of Illinois Press, 1979.

Worcester, Don, ed. *Pioneer Trails West.* Caldwell, Idaho: Caxton Printers, 1985.

GUIDES, DIARIES, AND REMINISCENCES

Baker, Jean Rio. "By Windjammer and Prairie Schooner London to Salt Lake City." In *Covered Wagon Women*, Vol. 3. Edited by Kenneth Holmes. Glendale, Calif.: Arthur Clark, 1984.

Bruff, J. Goldsborough. *Gold Rush: The Journals, Drawings, and Other Papers of J. Goldsborough Bruff.* Edited by Georgia Willis Read and Ruth Gaines. New York: Columbia University Press, 1949.

Bryant, Edwin. *What I Saw in California.* New York: D. Appleton, 1848. Reprint, Minneapolis: Ross and Haines, 1967.

Buckingham, Harriet Talcott. "Crossing the Plains in 1851." In *Covered Wagon Women*, Vol 3. Edited by Kenneth Holmes. Glendale, Calif.: Arthur Clark, 1984.

Child, Andrew. *Overland Route to California.* Milwaukee: Daily Sentinel Steam Power Press, 1852.

Clark, Caroline Hopkins. "Liverpool to Utah in 1866 by Sailing Ship and Prairie Schooner." In *Covered Wagon Women*, Vol. 9. Edited by Kenneth Holmes. Spokane, Wash.: Arthur Clark, 1990.

Clayton, William. *The Latter-Day Saints Emigrants' Guide.* St. Louis: Chambers and Knapp, 1848. Reprint, Gerald, Mo.: Patrice Press, 1983.

Clayton, William. *The Journal of William Clayton.* Salt Lake City: Daughters of Utah Pioneers, 1994.

Clayton, William. *William Clayton's Journal.* Salt Lake City: Deseret News, 1921.

Clyman, James. *Journal of a Mountain Man.* Edited by Linda M. Hasselstrom. Missoula: Mountain Press Publishing, 1984.

Cummings, Mariett Foster. "A Trip across the Continent." In *Covered Wagon Women,* Vol. 4. Edited by Kenneth Holmes. Glendale, Calif.: Arthur Clark, 1985.

Frémont, John Charles. *The Exploring Expedition to the Rocky Mountains.* Washington, D.C.: Gales and Seaton, 1845. Reprint, Washington, D.C.: Smithsonian Institution Press, 1988.

Goodridge, Sohia Lois. "The Mormon Trail, 1850." In *Covered Wagon Women,* Vol. 2. Edited by Kenneth Holmes. Glendale, Calif.: Arthur Clark, 1983.

Hafen, Mary Ann. *Recollections of a Handcart Pioneer of 1860: A Woman's Life on the Mormon Frontier.* Lincoln: University of Nebraska Press, 1983.

Hastings, Lansford. *The Emigrants' Guide to Oregon and California.* 1845. Reprint, Princeton: Princeton University Press, 1932.

Horn, Hosea. *Horn's Overland Guide.* New York: J. H. Colton, 1853.

King, Hannah Tapfield. "My Journal." In *Covered Wagon Women,* Vol. 6. Edited by Kenneth Holmes. Glendale, Calif.: Arthur Clark, 1986.

Korns, Roderic, and Dale Morgan, eds. *West from Fort Bridger: The Pioneering of the Immigrant Trails across Utah, 1846–1850.* Revised by Will Bagley and Harold Schindler. Logan: Utah State University Press, 1994.

Lienhard, Heinrich. *From St. Louis to Sutter's Fort, 1846.* Edited by Erwin and Elisabeth Gudde. Norman: University of Oklahoma Press, 1961.

Lightner, Mary Elizabeth. "Journal of a Mormon Woman, 1863." In *Covered Wagon Women,* Vol. 8. Edited by Kenneth Holmes. Glendale, Calif.: Arthur Clark, 1989.

Little, James A. *From Kirtland to Salt Lake City.* Salt Lake City: James Little, 1890.

Madsen, Susan Arrington. *I Walked to Zion: True Stories of Young Pioneers on the Mormon Trail.* Salt Lake City: Deseret Book Company, 1994.

Mitchell, S. Augustus. *A New Map of Texas, Oregon, and California.* Reprint, Oakland: Biobooks, 1948.

Morgan, Dale. *Overland in 1846.* Georgetown, Calif.: Talisman Press, 1963.

Mousley, Sarah Maria. "Delaware to Utah, 1857." In *Covered Wagon Women*, Vol. 7. Edited by Kenneth Holmes. Glendale, Calif.: Arthur Clark, 1988.

Piercy, Frederick H. *Route from Liverpool to Great Salt Lake Valley*. Edited by Fawn M. Brodie. Cambridge: Belknap Press of Harvard University Press, 1962.

Piercy, Frederick H. *Route from Liverpool to Great Salt Lake Valley*. Edited by James Linforth. Liverpool: Franklin D. Richards, 1855.

Pratt, Sarah. "The Daily Notes of Sarah Pratt." In *Covered Wagon Women*, Vol. 4. Edited by Kenneth Holmes. Glendale, Calif.: Arthur Clark, 1985.

Sessions, Patty Bartlett. Diary. LDS Church Archives. Salt Lake City.

Sessions, Patty. "A Pioneer Mormon Diary." In *Covered Wagon Women*, Vol. 1. Edited by Kenneth Holmes. Glendale, Calif.: Arthur Clark, 1983.

Shackleford, Ruth. "To California by the Mormon Trail, 1865." In *Covered Wagon Women*, Vol. 9. Edited by Kenneth Holmes. Spokane, Wash.: Arthur Clark, 1990.

Stansbury, Howard. *An Expedition to the Valley of the Great Salt Lake of Utah*. Philadelphia: Lippincott, Grambo, 1852.

Wilkins, James F. *An Artist on the Overland Trail: The 1849 Diary and Sketches of James F. Wilkins*. Edited by John F. McDermott. San Marino, Calif.: Huntington Library, 1968.

BOOKLETS AND PAMPHLETS

"Fort Bridger/Pioneer Trail Tour." Utah Museum Volunteers Association. August 1, 1992.

"Fort Bridger." Wyoming Recreation Department, State Archives and Historical Department.

"Fort Caspar Museum." Casper, Wy.

"Fort Kearny." Nebraska State Historical Society. Ed. Leaflet No. 7.

"Fort Laramie." Washington, D.C.: National Park Service.

"Historic Nauvoo, Illinois." Nauvoo Tourism and Western Illinois Tourism Council.

"Landmarks and Events along the Historic Mormon Trail." Daughters of Utah Pioneers.

"Mormon Pioneer National Historic Trail." U.S. Department of the Interior, National Park Service, 1994.

"Nauvoo City Beautiful." Reorganized Church of Jesus Christ of Latter Day Saints.

"Nauvoo, the Beautiful and Historic Carthage Block." The Church of Jesus Christ of Latter-day Saints.

"Oregon Trail: Oregon National Historic Trail." U.S. Department of the Interior, 1993.

"Scotts Bluff." Washington, D.C.: National Park Service.

"Winter Quarters Historical Site and Mormon Pioneer Cemetery." The Church of Jesus Christ of Latter-day Saints.

Index